AF615594

Workbench Projects

Gamebird Trio

By Ernie Muehlmatt
with Ed Rogan

Editor
Daniel J. Marsteller

Editorial Assistant
Lori A. Jaymes

Advertising Manager
Diana Marcum

Design
CW Design Solutions, Inc.

Customer Accounts Manager
Kelly L. Mease

Administrative Assistant
Romayne F. Leedy

Publisher
J. Richard Noel

Chairman
M. David Detweiler

Store Sales (877) 544–4051

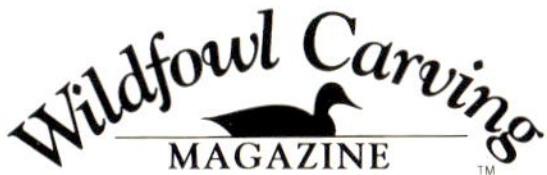

1300 MARKET ST., STE. 202
LEMOYNE, PA 17043–1420
717–234–5091, 717–234–1359 (FAX)

E-mail:
customerservice@wildfowl-carving.com

Website:
www.wildfowl-carving.com

WORKBENCH PROJECTS: GAMEBIRD TRIO was produced by the staff of WILDFOWL CARVING MAGAZINE: Daniel J. Marsteller, Editor; Lori A. Jaymes, Editorial Assistant; Diana Marcum, Advertising and Sales Manager; Kelly Mease, Customer Accounts Manager; J. Richard Noel, Publisher; M. David Detweiler, Chairman.

From the Editor

Thank you for purchasing WORKBENCH PROJECTS: GAMEBIRD TRIO. For those of you who are unaware, the WORKBENCH PROJECTS series is published by WILDFOWL CARVING MAGAZINE, the only magazine in the world devoted exclusively to bird carving. The idea for this book featuring gamebirds came directly from subscribers to the magazine, whom we surveyed as to their preferences of bird species over the past year. Traditionally, upland gamebirds have been somewhat overlooked by the bird carving community, which tends to be dominated by the good-natured debate between decoy and songbird carvers, respectively; that is why it came as a surprise to us at WILDFOWL CARVING that gamebird species, which do not fit neatly into either one of these groups, were the most sought-after birds in our surveys. So, toward the end of satisfying our public's thirst for gamebird instruction, we offer in these pages carving demonstrations on three members of the family: the American woodcock, the bobwhite quail, and the eastern ruffed grouse.

At the helm of this ship is the able Captain Ernie Muehlmatt, a veteran of more than 30 years' wildfowl carving experience, and a World Champion at the Ward World Championship Wildfowl Carving Competition three times over. A highly respected teacher as well as carver, Muehlmatt documents his artistic process with a sturdy but informal hand, urging his students and readers to use the trial-and-error technique and to play around with their tools and paints, through which endeavors he hopes they will grasp the effectiveness of each tool and glean a better understanding of the possibilities of bird carving as a whole. Instrumental in Ernie's work is his employment of the one-piece sculpturing method, in which he contends that the shape of the wood often lends itself to certain designs, in effect "telling" the carver how to proceed. If this idea sounds mystical in a way, perhaps it is; after all, bird carvers are dealing in the creation of art.

Now it is time for the editor to stand aside and let the author have ado with his readers, so the torch of carving knowledge can be passed from one generation to the next, and with it, all the peculiar joys and frustrations held within. As you begin, I'd like to join Mr. Muehlmatt in reminding you that carving is meant to be a relaxing process, a leisure-time activity, so don't become discouraged too easily if your first carving does not turn out to your liking. Chances are, the next one will be a good deal better.

Contents

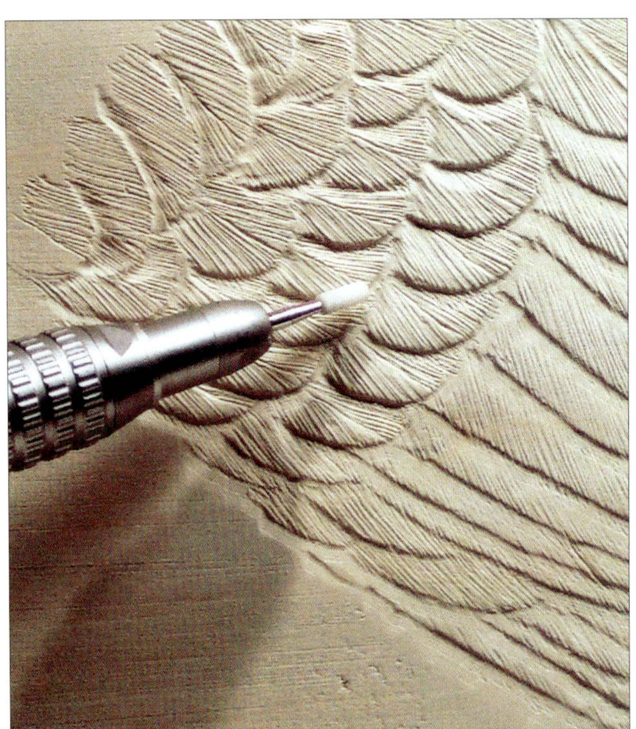

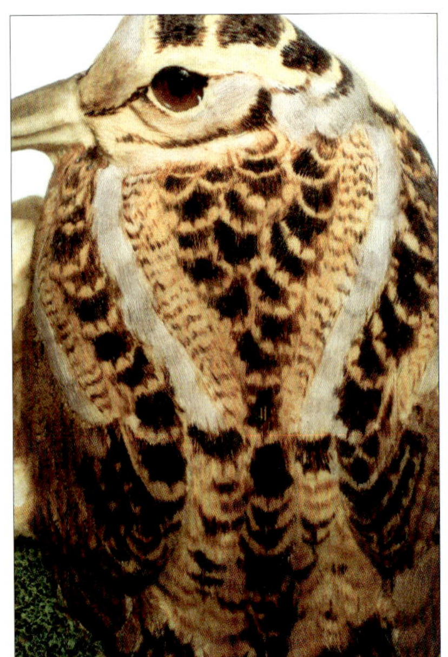

The American Woodcock

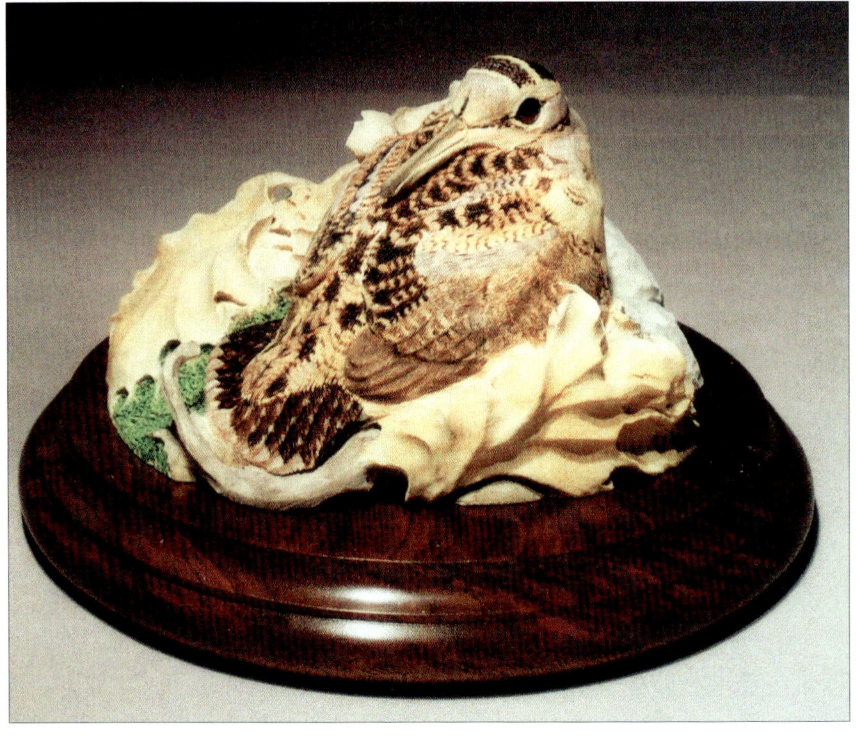

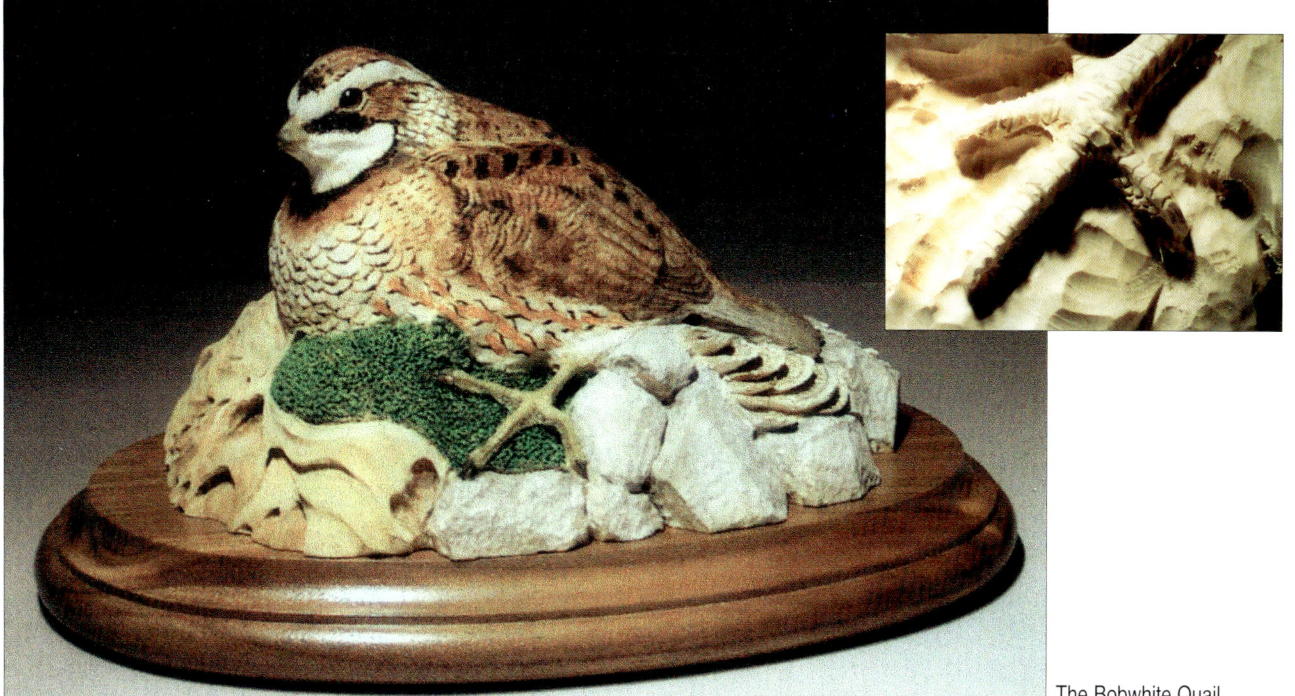

The Bobwhite Quail

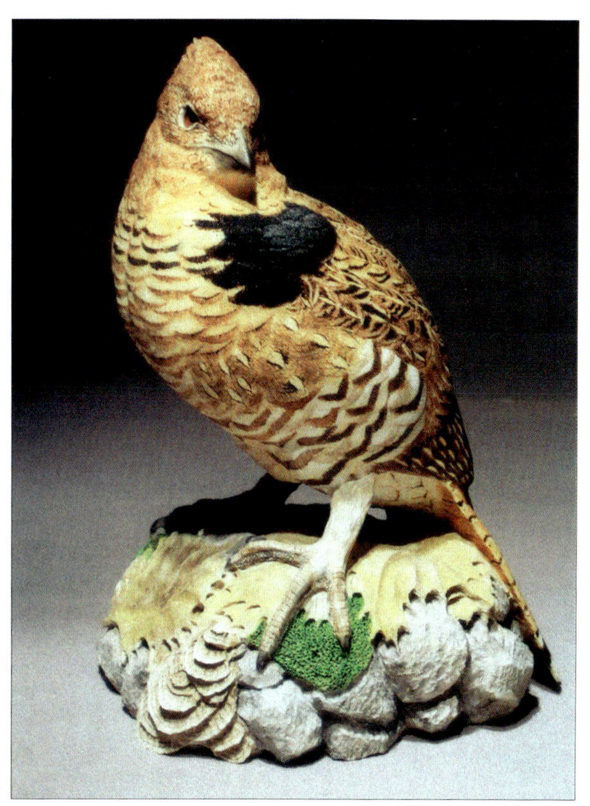

The Eastern Ruffed Grouse

INTRODUCTION

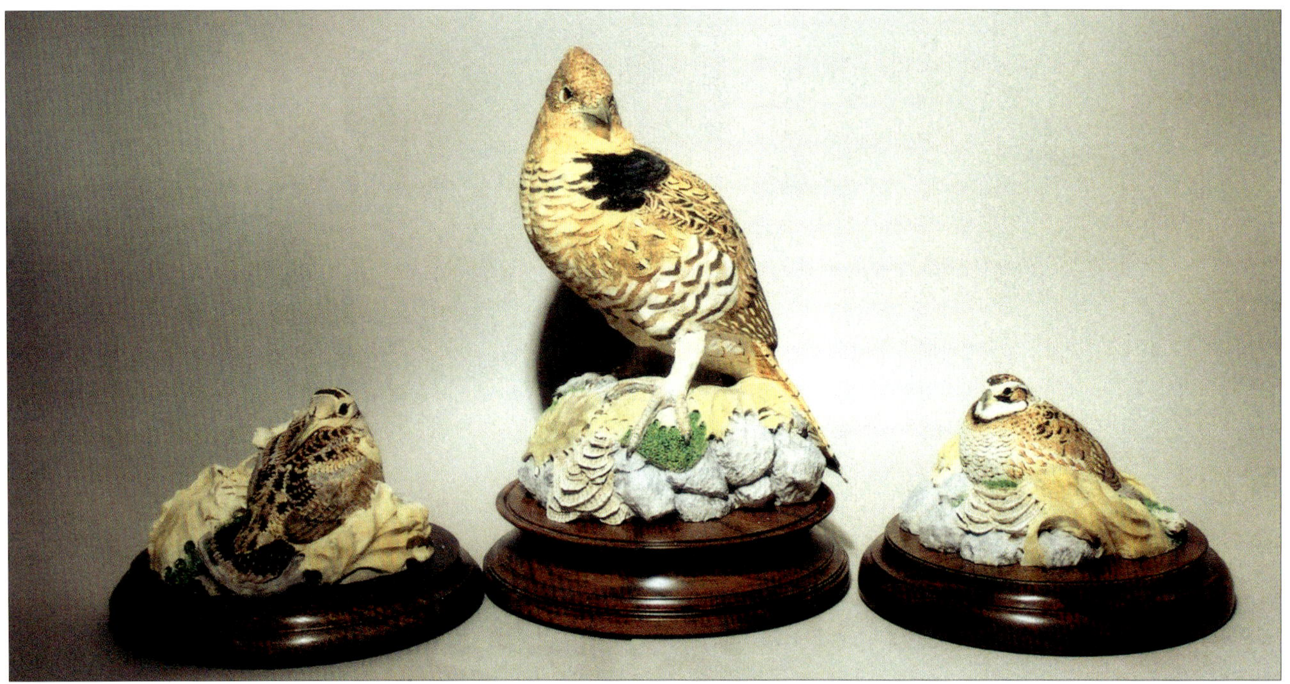

The Gamebird Trio. From left: the American woodcock, the eastern ruffed grouse, and the bobwhite quail.

Over the past 25 years I have prepared carving projects for seminars with the goal of encouraging the creative minds of my students as my number one priority. I have covered all types of birds in these seminars, from songbirds to raptors to the woodland gamebirds discussed in this book. I have also experimented with many different arrangements and themes within my work, but in recent years one-piece sculptures have become my particular specialty. The one-piece method of carving can be challenging at first, and anyone who attempts it will have his or her share of setbacks and frustrations, but in my experience, and hopefully in yours, the sense of achievement resulting from the finished product rewards the ego handsomely for any difficulties encountered during the carving process.

Prior to 1970 no one dreamed of creating a realistic one-piece wood sculpture with habitat because the tools necessary to make the process work were simply not available. This changed over the following decade with the development of such tools as Foredom flexible-shaft grinders, burning pens, high-speed grinders, and diamond ruby bits. These and other technological breakthroughs worked sufficiently well in the manipulation of carving woods such as tupelo and basswood that carvers became able to reproduce the finest details of live birds in their work. This technological progression led naturally to the highly detailed, intricate, and incredibly lifelike style of decorative bird carving that has come to define the state of the art form as it stands today.

The Ward World Championship Wildfowl Carving Competition was inaugurated in 1971, and the event has been held every year since, through 2005. If you visit the Roland E. Powell Convention Center in Ocean City this year, you will be able to observe the evolution of the art of bird carving firsthand. Part of the allure of this show, and bird carving shows in general, is that all styles and genres are represented somewhere on the tables. You can still find the traditional hunting decoy, with its clean, simple lines, that set the wheels in motion, and beside it you can see the detailed decorative carving, as scrupulous as Mother Nature in its rendering of every feather.

My intent in writing this book is not necessarily for all of its readers to become champion wildfowl carvers, but rather to offer those with an interest in gamebirds and art a chance to try their hands at recreating these handsome species in wood, keeping squarely in mind that any mistakes made will be in the interest of improvement, and that the primary goal is to have fun. I would advise you to read the entire book through before beginning to carve, because the techniques used in creating these three gamebirds overlap a good deal, and you will be better prepared to execute your first project after you have an overview of the information and advice offered here concerning all three.

CARVING A ONE-PIECE SCULPTURE

All three of the birds in this book were carved using the one-piece method. One-piece carvings require a significant roughing-out phase. A rule that I have developed from experience is that faster removal of wood will produce a looser bird and slower removal a tighter piece. When you work too slowly you lose your sense of the direction or the focus on your overall strategy for the carving process. That is not to say that you should rush, simply that you should take advantage of your own momentum; more often than not it will take you in the right direction.

The initial cutout photos of these birds show multiple cuts with a band saw. Unless you are capable of using a band saw at various angles I would remind you that the same results can be achieved by using a Kutzall bit in a flexible-shaft machine. It may take longer and produce more dust but your fingers will be safer. When you have the initial patterns cut out, start roughing out the bill, then the head, cape, body, wings, tail, and feet. Habitat should be attempted last, especially by the beginner. The texturing on the birds in this project was stoned and then burned for color, so try to match the color of the burning as well as that of the painting in the photos. When you are ready to carve habitat, a stump, rock, moss, leaves, lichens, and so on can be carved with the same tools used for the bird. Photos and text will be used to illustrate the various procedures.

One-piece carvings encourage the imagination to explore carving techniques that put animation into the sculpture. While certain anatomical correctness is required, for which the carver should pay close attention to his or her reference material, he or she should relax and not feel the same pressures experienced by carvers preparing a piece for competition. Remember, the important thing is the appeal of the finished composition as a whole.

CARVING MATERIALS

- Carving blocks (see pages 9, 34, and 56 for sizes)
- Glass eyes (see pages 9, 34, and 56 for sizes)
- Flexible-shaft machine
- High-speed micromotor machine
- Various carving bits
- Woodburning system
- Various burning bits
- Sandpaper
- Pencil
- Cyanoacrylate (CA) glue
- Baking soda
- Reference material (see page 72)

Shown here are the bits and sanding mandrel I used in the carving of the three birds in this book. I used the Kutzall in a Foredom flexible-shaft machine and the grinders and other bits in a high-speed micromotor machine. Note: All of the bits can be used in either machine; both machines are not required.

a. Kutzall
b. Flat-end stump-cutter
c. Round stump-cutter
d. Ruby stone
e. Bullet diamond
f. Sanding mandrel
g. Bullet diamond
h. Diamond ball
i. Diamond flame
j. Moss cutter (needle diamond bit, for habitat)
k. Tapered medium-grit diamond needle bit (for making rock crevices)

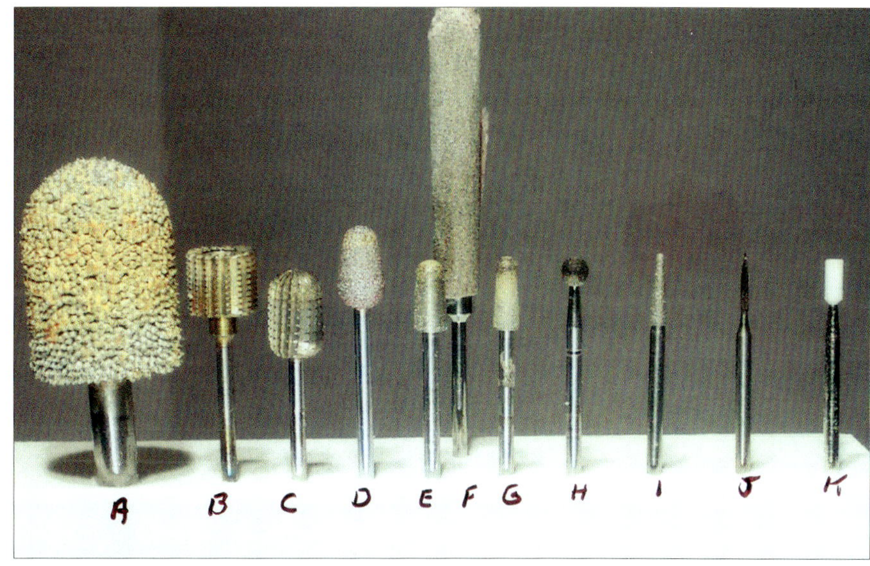

PAINTING A ONE-PIECE SCULPTURE

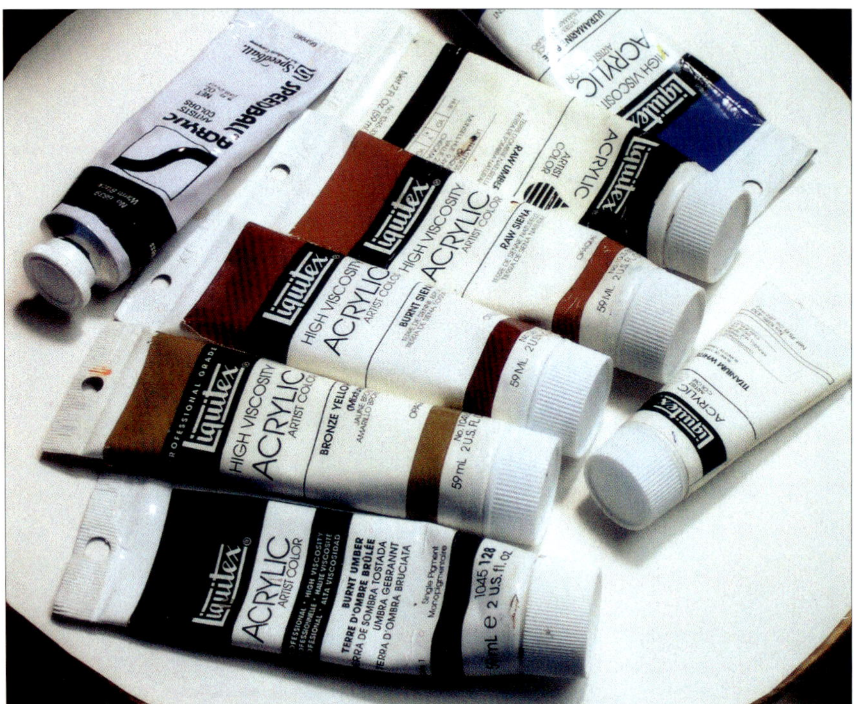

Here are the paints that are used on the upland gamebirds.

We all struggle with painting. I have been painting all my life and I still have difficulty. I have worked out my own simplified system of painting that I call the limited, or muted, palette. On my muted palette color wheel, I have three colors that can be used to paint half of the birds that I do.

On a regular color wheel we have yellow, red, and blue. With these three colors, any other color can be mixed. Any time you mix two colors that are directly opposite each other on the color wheel, the resulting color is gray or black. For instance, green is a mixture of yellow and blue that are adjacent to each other on the color wheel. Directly across from green is red. Mix green and red in equal parts, and the resulting color is black. Blue and red are adjacent to each other on the wheel. If you mix red and blue you get violet. If you go across the wheel to yellow and mix yellow with violet you get black. The same thing happens when you mix yellow and red to make orange. Mix orange with blue (which is directly across the color wheel) and you get black. If you were to paint a cardinal and it was too bright red, you could mix a little green with the red to tone it down.

On a muted palette of yellow, red, and green, I use raw umber or burnt umber for yellow, burnt sienna (a red brown) for red, and ultramarine blue for blue. I mix no other colors or white with them. Using these three colors, ultramarine blue, raw or burnt umber, and burnt sienna, one can paint a chickadee, nuthatch, bluebird, woodcock, grouse, quail, wrens, most owls, and many birds of prey. Several years ago I carved five prairie falcons on a rock setting. The piece—the birds and habitat—was painted with only two colors, burnt umber mixed with ultramarine blue, and white.

In my technique the colors are used as light washes. To mix a wash, start with a bit of pigment the size of a pea and a tablespoon of water. After this is thoroughly mixed add more water until you have the desired strength. The washes should be transparent. I allow each wash to dry before applying another. One wash is applied on top of another until the desired tone of color or intensity is achieved. It is like applying colored sheets of film one on top of another until a desired tone is achieved. For example, a blue wash put on top of a brown wash will give you a grayer brown. A brown wash applied over a blue wash will give you a grayer blue. Most of the time no white is used. The white is applied first as gesso on selective parts of each bird.

One good way to learn how to paint is to sit down with a large sheet of white board and just mix colors, either thick or as washes, and see what happens. Vary the consistency of the paint with more or less water to see what that will do. Put washes of color on top of each other to see the results. Apply color on a wet surface and then on a dry surface to see

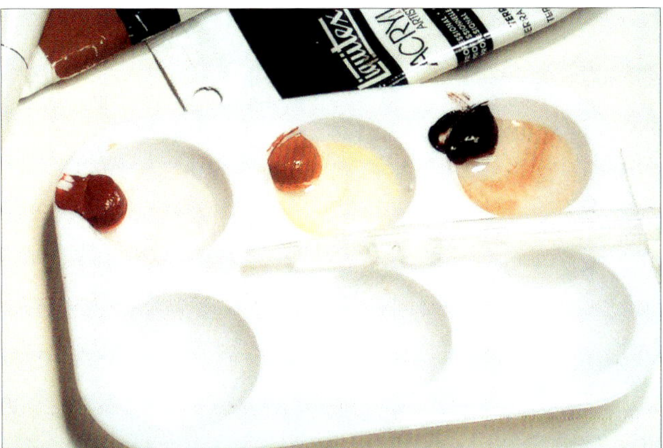

A pea-size amount of pigment is initially mixed with a tablespoon of water.

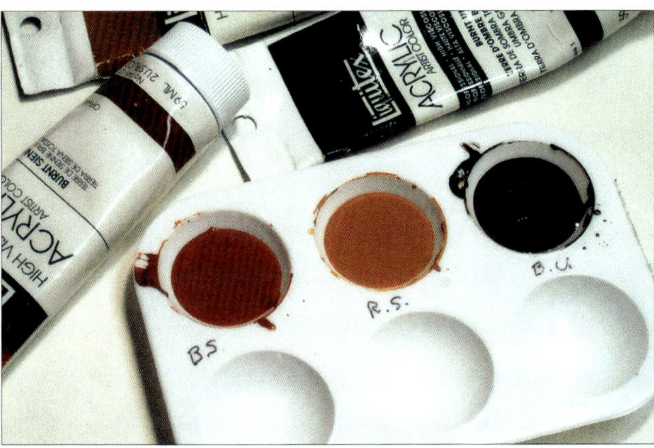

The resulting mixture is further diluted with water before application.

PAINTING MATERIALS

PAINTS

Jo Sonja's

- Gesso
- Titanium White
- Warm White
- Raw Umber
- Burnt Umber
- Burnt Sienna
- Raw Sienna
- Moss Green
- Cadmium Yellow Medium

Liquitex

- Ultramarine Blue
- Bronze Yellow

Speedball

- Warm Black

BRUSHES

- Yarka brushes #1–#5 (available from Knotts' Knives)
- Loew-Cornell Ultra 7020 #2–#4, #6
- Liquitex 1/2" Kolinsky Oval Wash

the results. Apply colors on top of black or white to see what happens. You can learn a great deal this way and not be afraid of learning on a carved bird. It is not so much learning how to paint as it is learning how to apply paint to the bird in the right consistency for the effect you want. Have fun with your practice board. There you can make all the mistakes you want.

In my experience, most mistakes in painting are made by applying too much paint or getting a color too dark. Always apply paint as watery washes, building up color slowly, a little at a time. Watch the results as you go along. If a bluebird is getting too blue, try a brown wash. Always stop applying washes one wash before you think you should. As tempting as it may be, don't apply that last wash. Remember, fear stifles creativity. Practice, play, and have fun. The photos on this page show the paints used and the process of mixing them.

All birds are sealed with a mixture of 50% lacquer and 50% lacquer thinner prior to the application of washes. The paint swatches on the following page demonstrate the color washes applied on the American woodcock, ruffed grouse, and bobwhite quail and how repeated washes increase the intensity of the color.

The carving and painting techniques used on the birds are similar. In addition to the birds themselves, woodland habitat also provides opportunities for creative minds. The palette for the habitat, like that of the birds, consists of the earth colors (umbers and siennas), ultramarine blue, white, black, yellow, and green.

PAINT SWATCHES

Burnt Umber

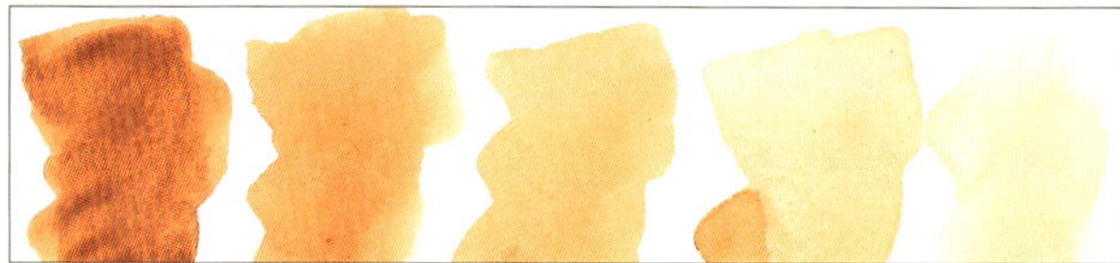

Raw Sienna

Raw Umber

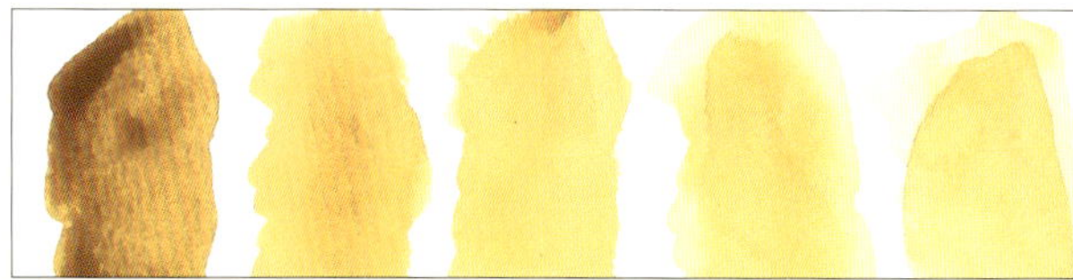

Bronze Yellow

Burnt Sienna

Ultramarine Blue

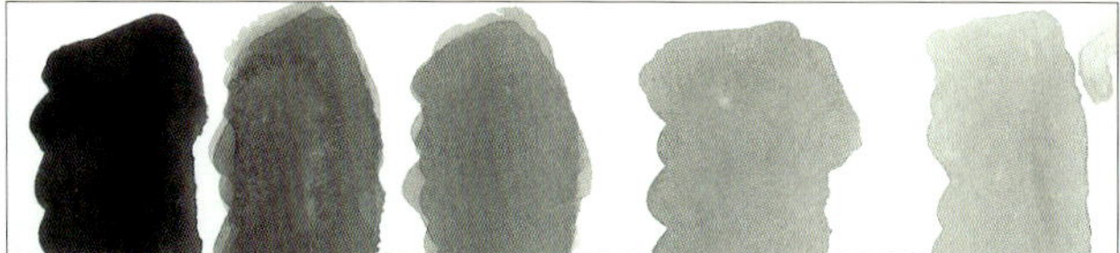

Warm Black

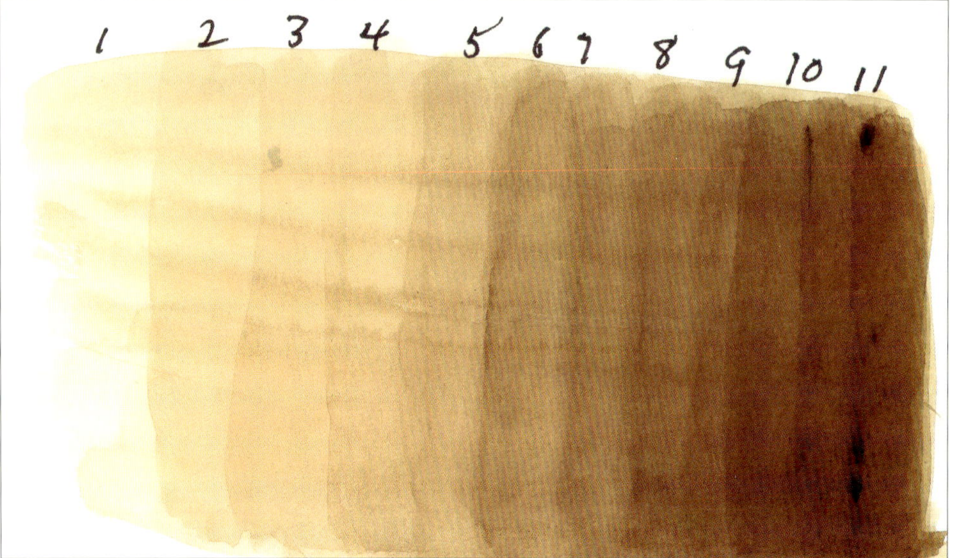

This swatch shows the gradation of layers of Burnt Umber washes. Use this technique of layering washes to achieve the desired colors on your birds.

THE AMERICAN WOODCOCK

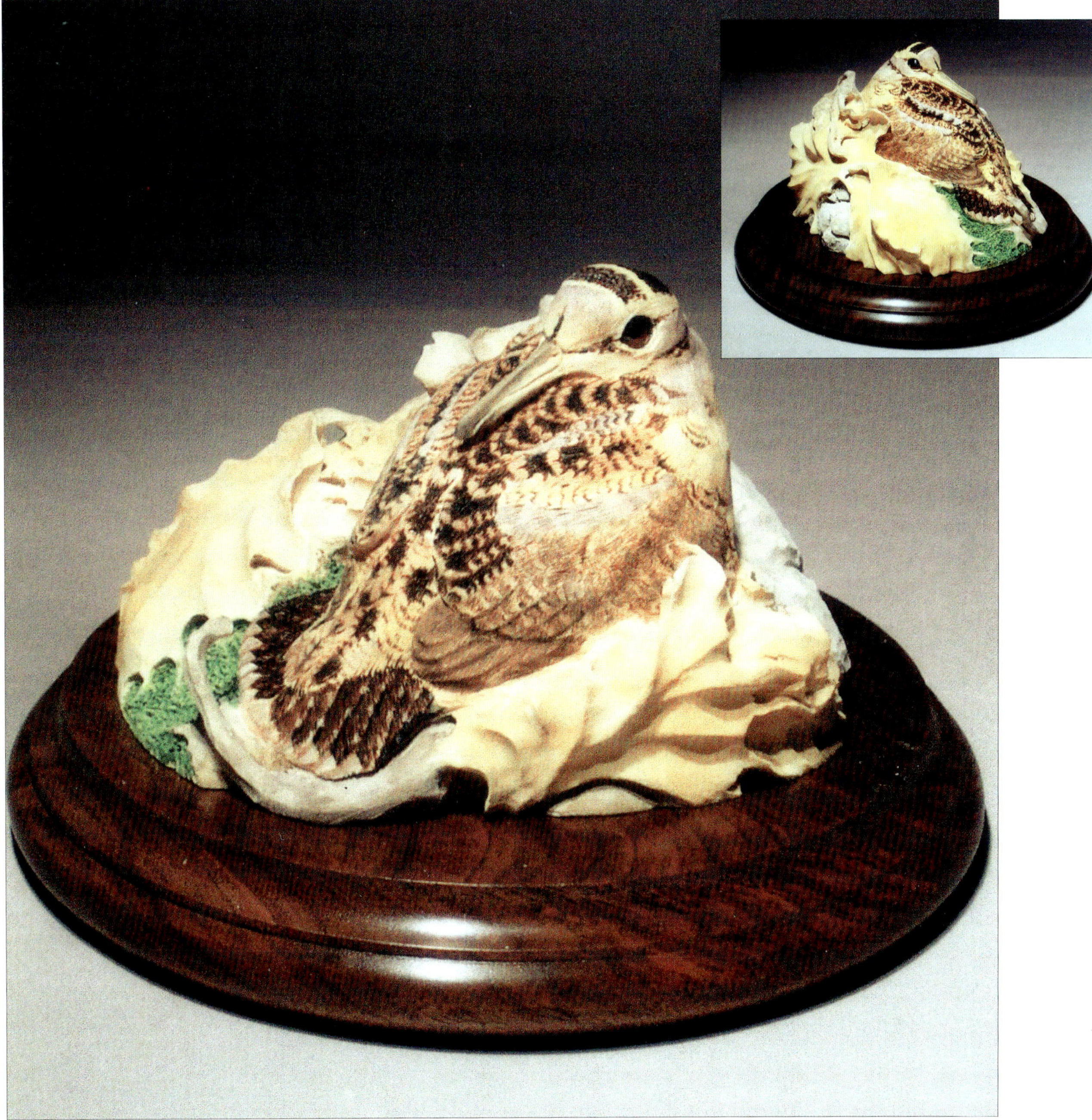

The completed American Woodcock.

The American woodcock is commonly found in the United States east of the Mississippi River and in Canada. The birds range in length from 10 to 12 inches and have conspicuous eyes set in the center of a large head. This unusual placement of the eyes enables the woodcock to view a 360-degree range of its environment. During daylight hours these birds tend to blend in with leaves and brush; at night they feed, plunging their long bills into moist ground groping for earthworms and grubs. Their courtship ritual, involving spiraling flight patterns, is particularly dramatic. Although technically classified as shorebirds, woodcocks have more in common with gamebirds; they have similar plumage and reside in the same mountain-woodland habitat. To carve this bird you will need a 10- x 6- x 6-inch block of tupelo or other carving wood, and a set of 10-millimeter dark brown glass eyes.

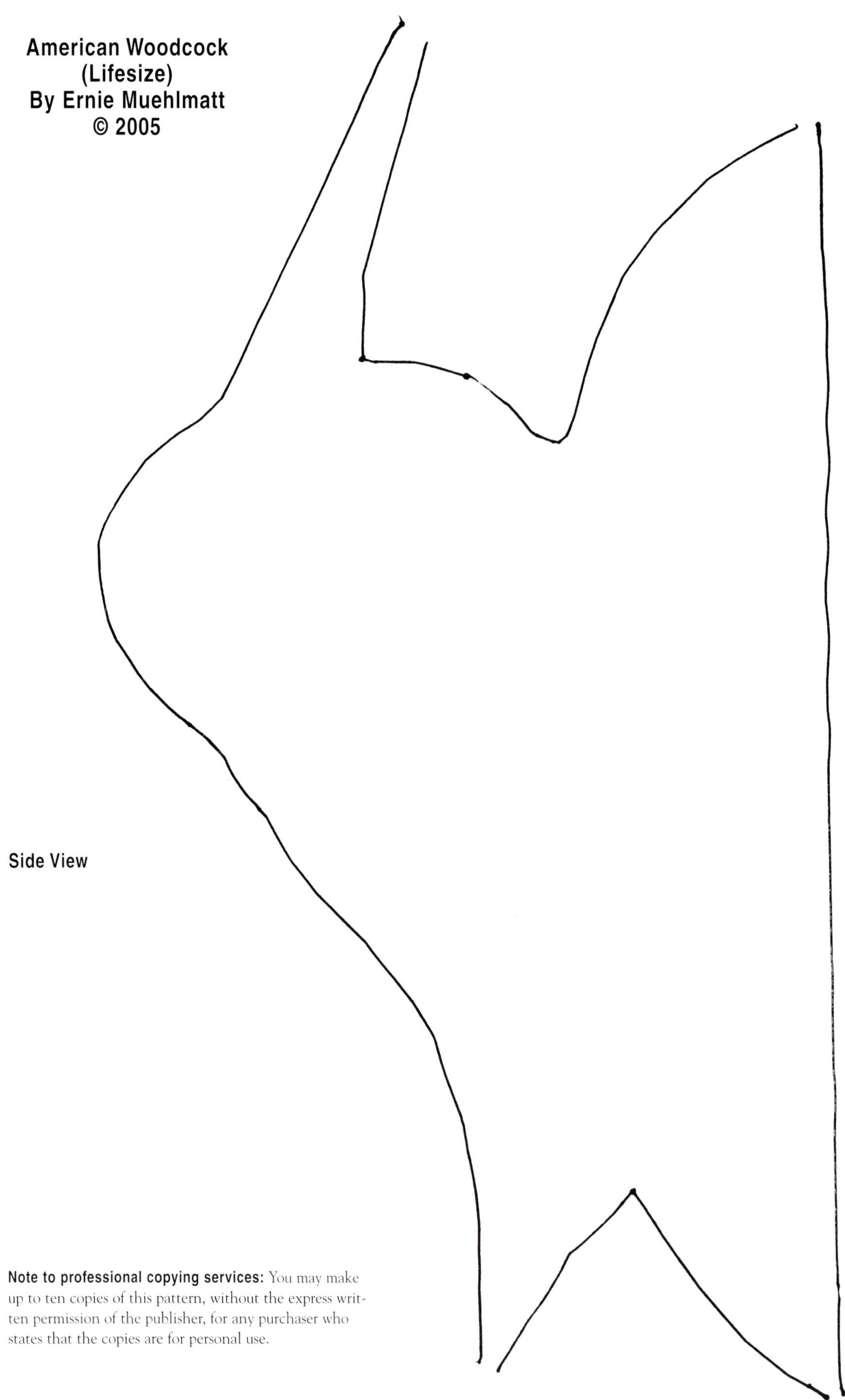
American Woodcock
(Lifesize)
By Ernie Muehlmatt
© 2005
Side View

Top View

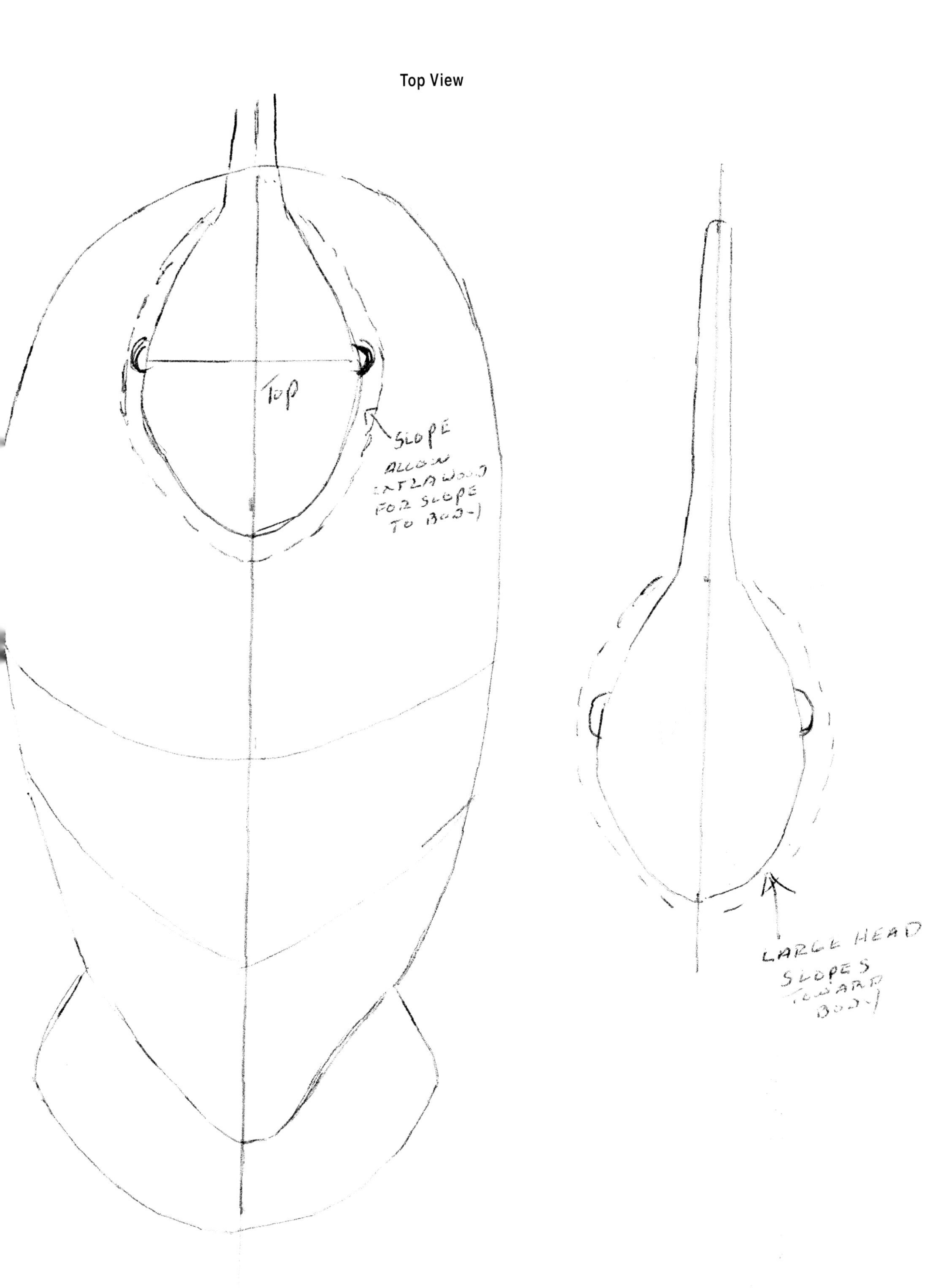

Top
SLOPE
ALLOW EXTRA WOOD FOR SLOPE TO BODY
LARGE HEAD SLOPES TOWARD BODY

Bill Reference

- Bills over 72 mm are always female
- Bills under 64 mm are always male
- Bills between 64 mm and 66 mm were males 95% of the time
- Birds with bills 67 mm to 69 mm were evenly divided

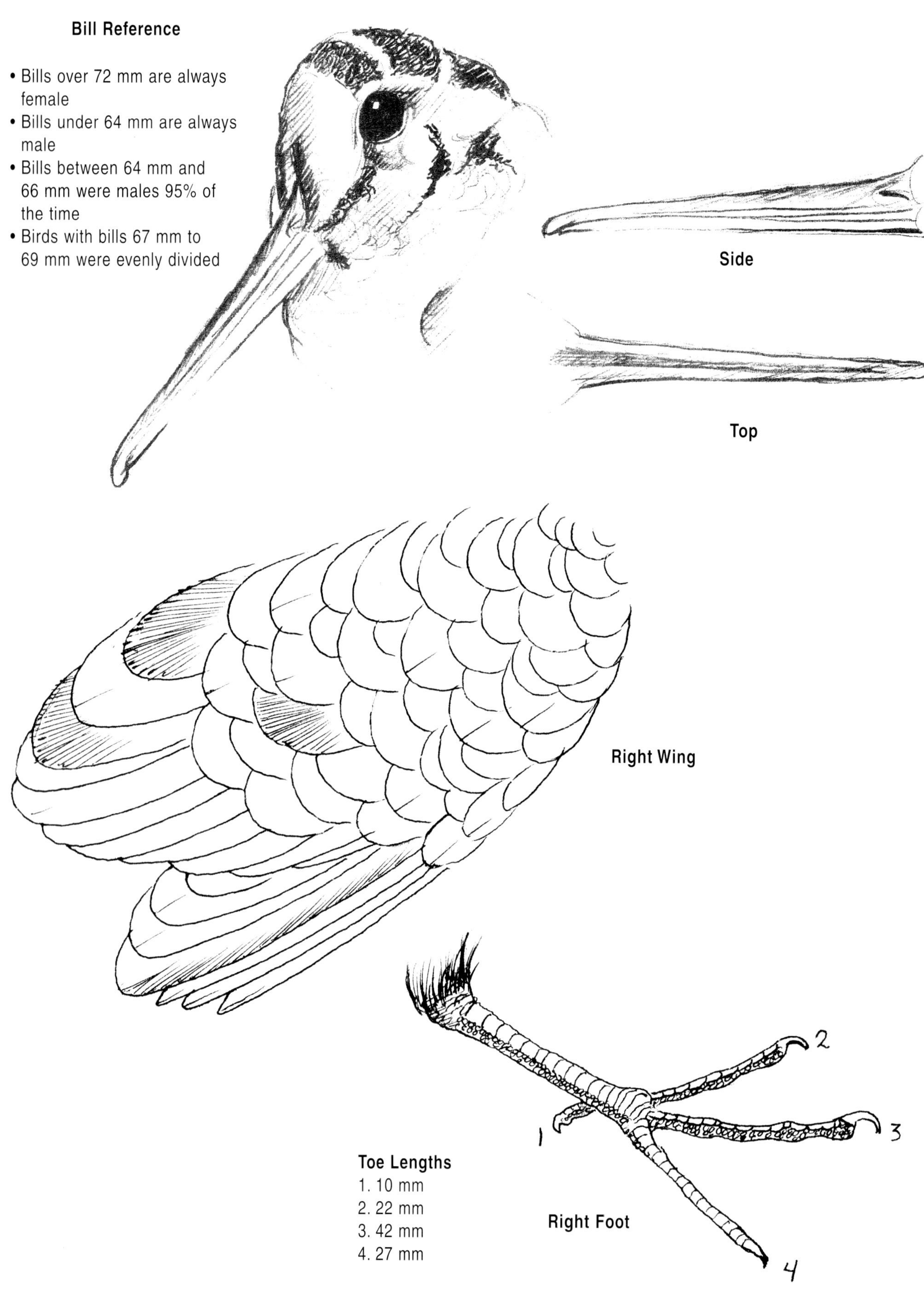

Toe Lengths

1. 10 mm
2. 22 mm
3. 42 mm
4. 27 mm

Left Wing

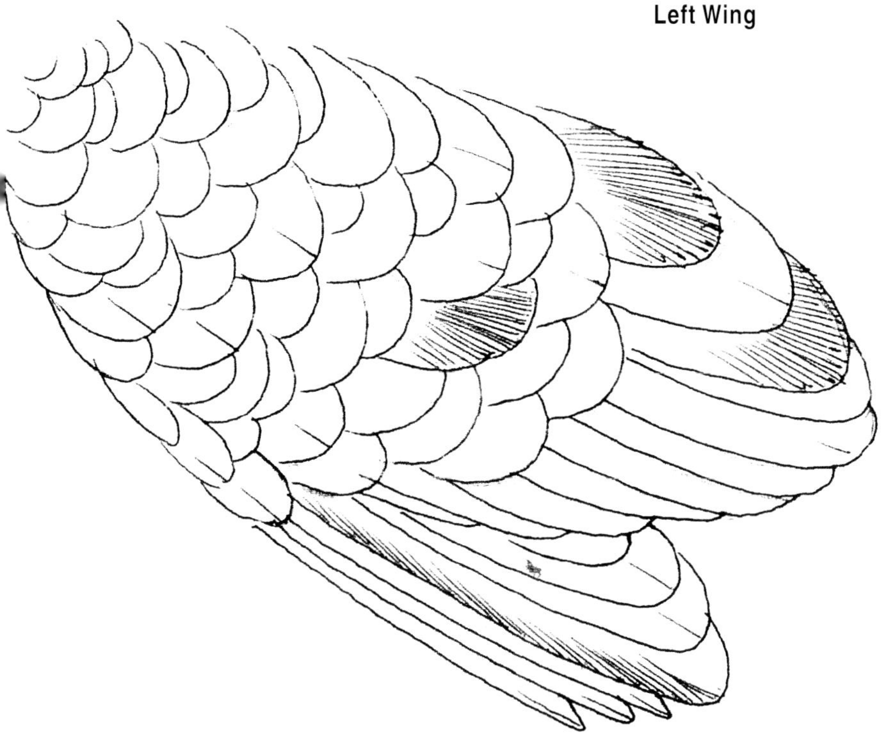

Left Foot

Toe Lengths

1. 10 mm
2. 22 mm
3. 42 mm
4. 27 mm

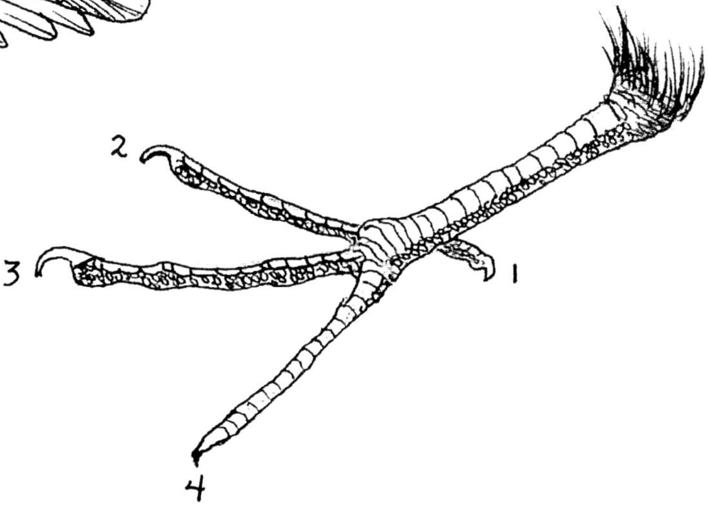

Head Reference—Side View

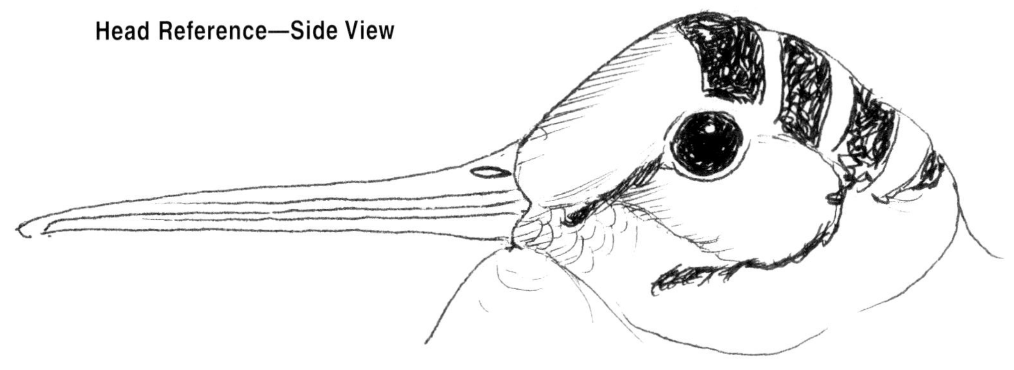

Head Reference—Top View

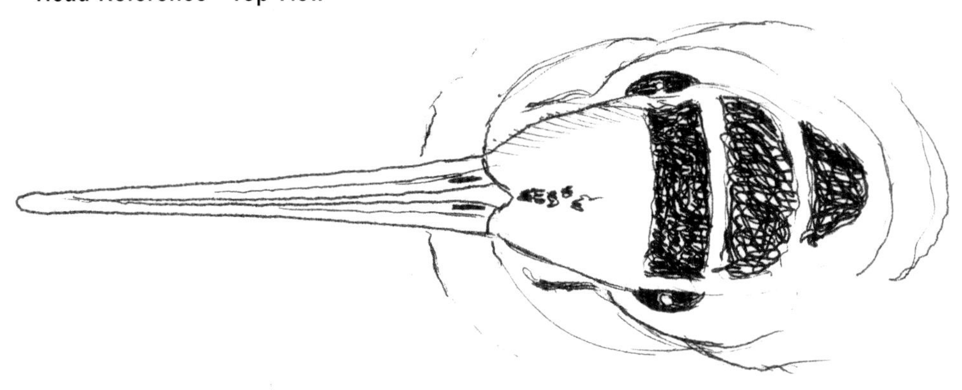

Head Reference—Front View

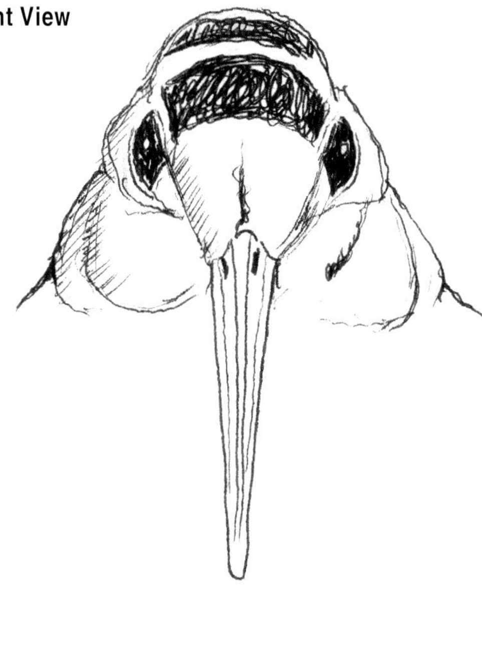

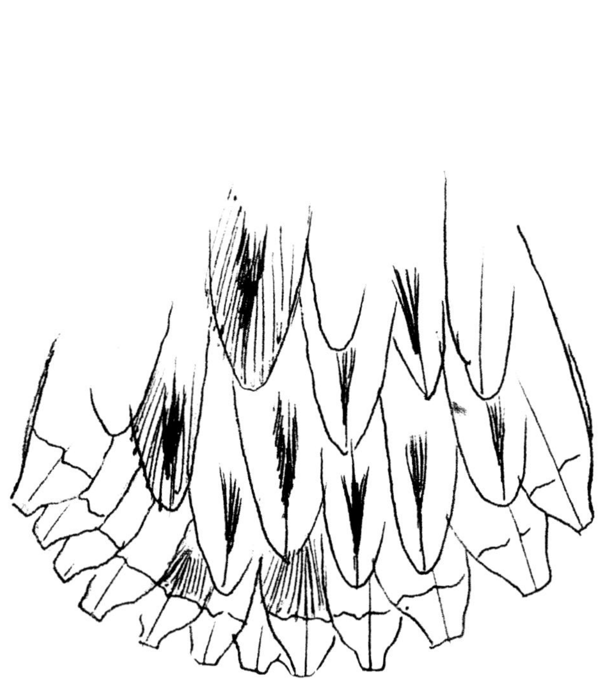

Tail Underside

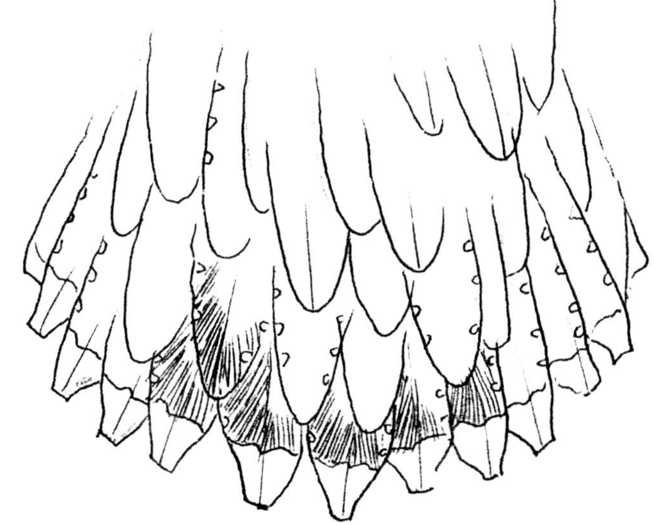

Tail Top Side

CARVING THE AMERICAN WOODCOCK

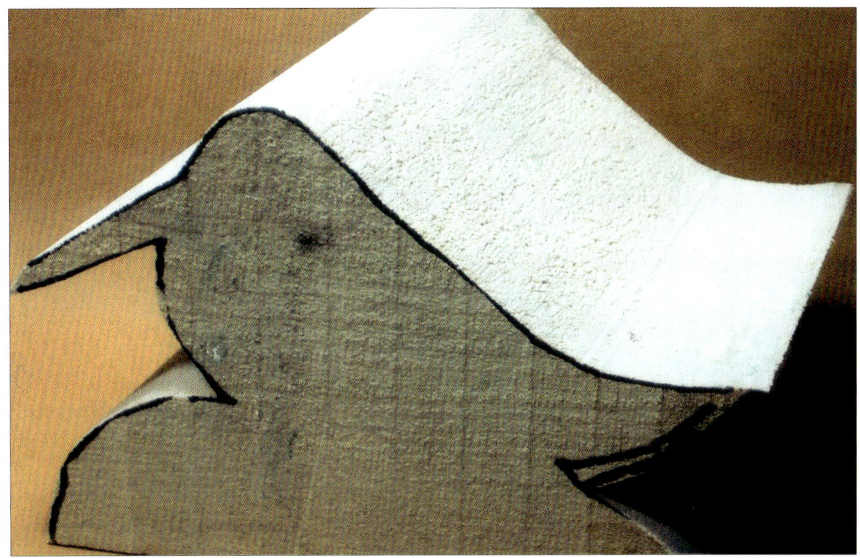

1 Cut out the side profile of the woodcock on a band saw.

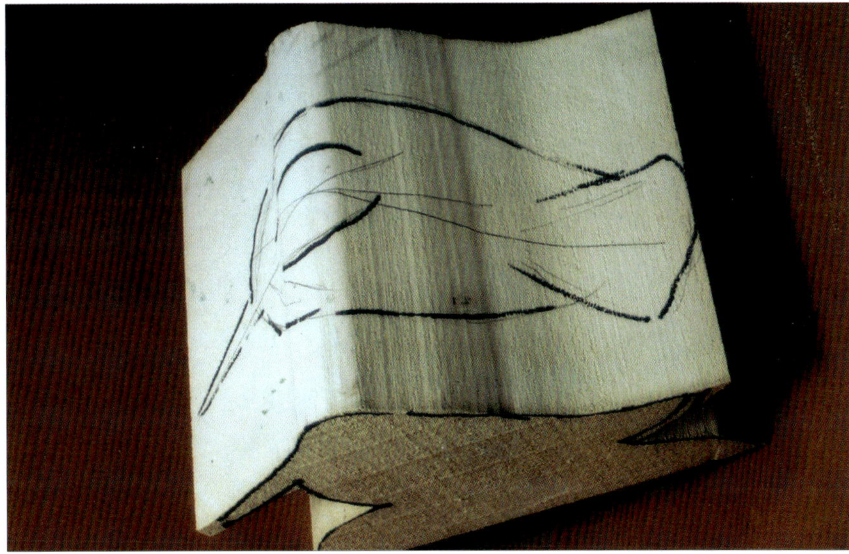

2 Outline the top pattern on the block and cut it out as well.

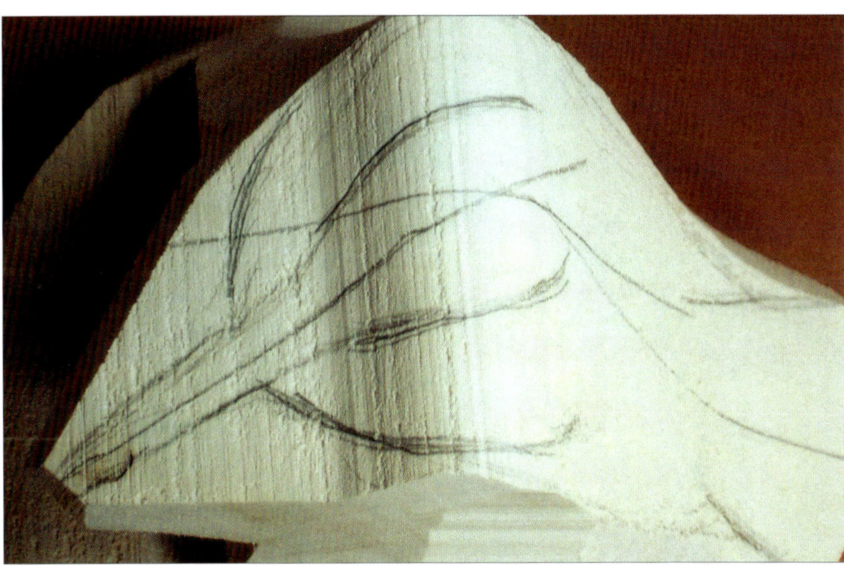

3 Remove wood slowly and carefully from the head and sides of the woodcock with a stump-cutter (in whichever grinder you have) after penciling in the head, bill, and centerlines as shown.

4 Rough out the head, bill, and chest with the stump-cutter as shown, leaving a bit of extra wood particularly around the bill.

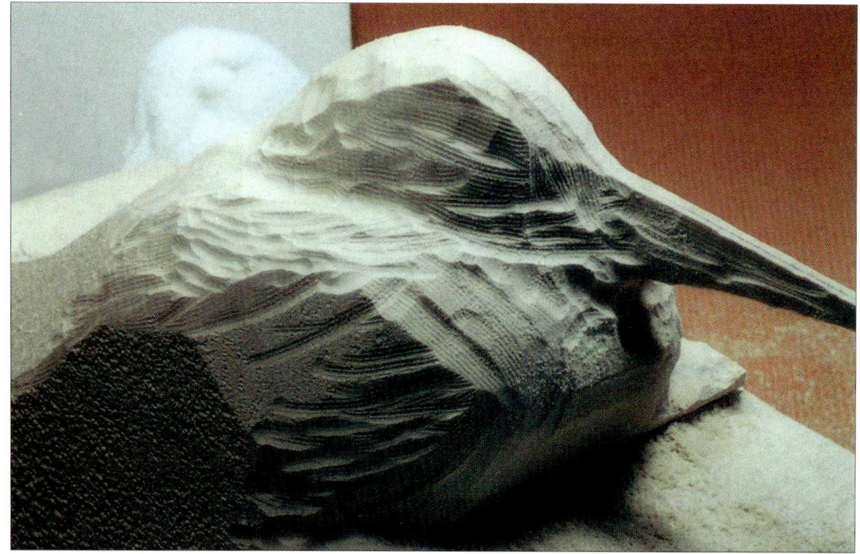

5 Shape the breast down to the underbelly, still using the stump-cutter.

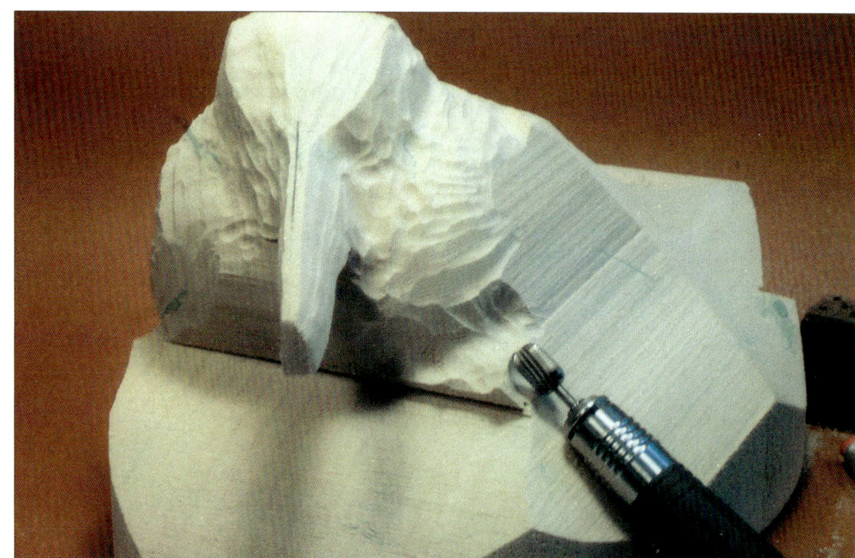

6 Shape the bill and forehead to approximate size with an 8-millimeter stump-cutter or a 5-millimeter diamond bullet, using a study bill and/or the measurements on page 12 for reference. I would advise saving the final shaping of the bill until the rest of the roughing-out process is complete, especially if you are a beginner, to prevent accidental breakage of the bill. Either way, when you have attained the final shape of the bill, cover it with instant cyanoacrylate (CA) glue for added strength.

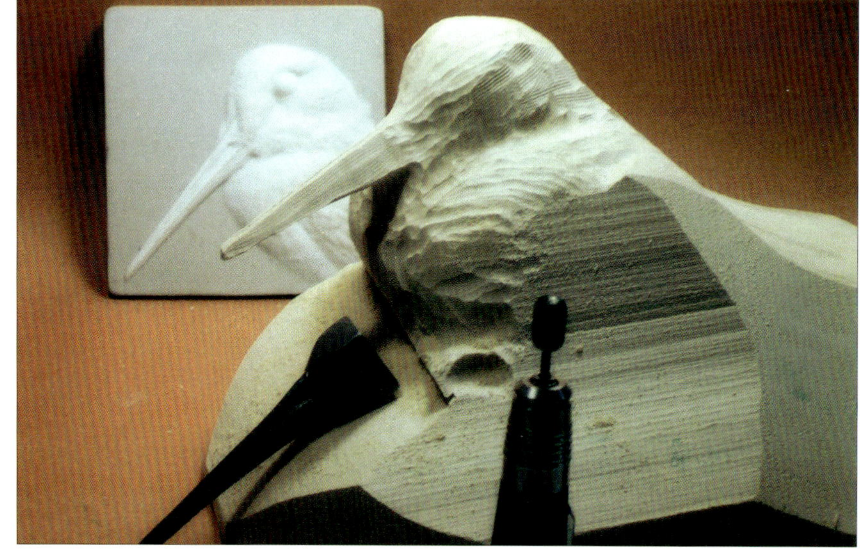

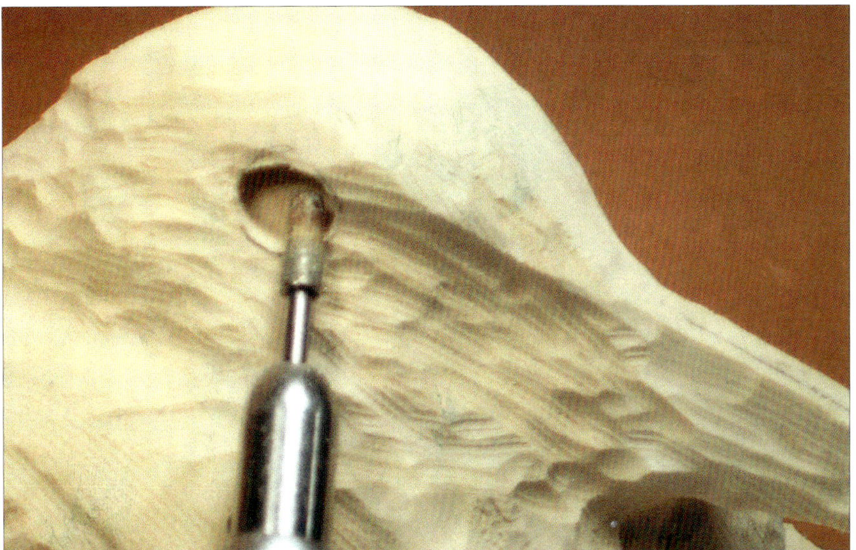

7 Shape the eye socket with a 3- or 4-millimeter diamond bullet, first marking in the position after consulting your reference material for measurements. The woodcock requires 10-millimeter dark brown glass eyes, but for now just draw in and carve approximately a 9-millimeter-wide, 3-millimeter-deep circular hole.

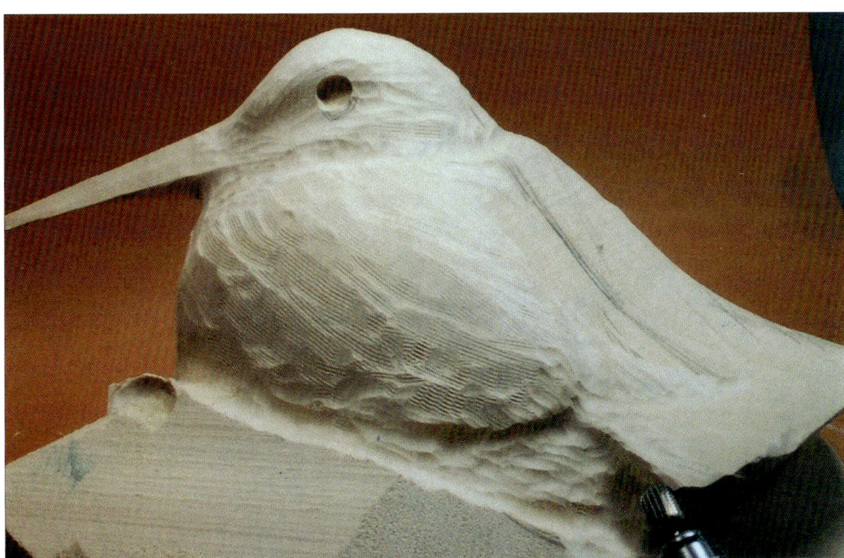

8 Continue shaping the body with the stump-cutter using your reference material to guide your cuts.

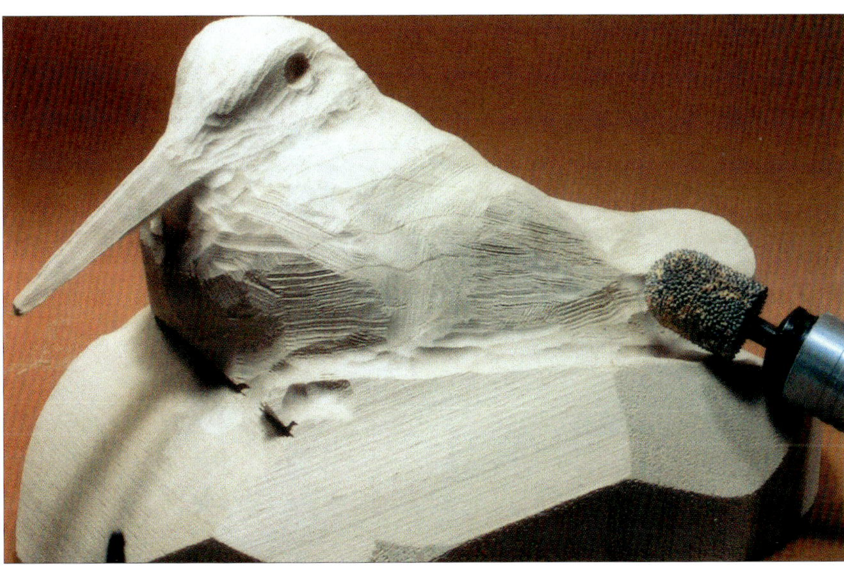

9 Contour the major wing-feather groups with the stump-cutter. Smooth any edges or depressions with a 4-millimeter pear-shaped ruby cutter, then sand the area either by hand or with the aid of a mandrel.

10 Use a Kutzall bit to rough-shape the habitat/base.

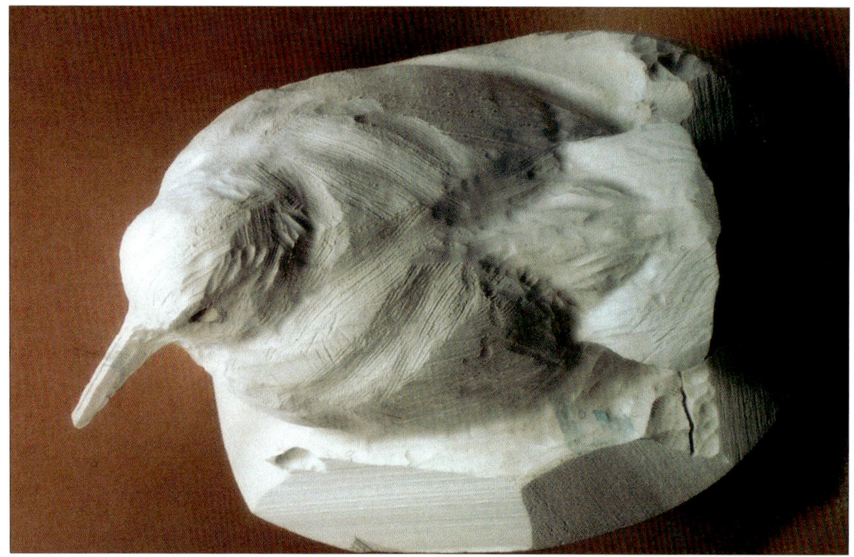

11 Bring the bill down to its final size at this point. Carve the ridge on the upper mandible $2\frac{1}{2}$ millimeters wide and $3\frac{1}{2}$ millimeters deep. This can be done with a 3-millimeter bullet or a 4-millimeter pear-shaped diamond. The separation of the upper and lower mandibles can be defined with a small, pointed burning tip.

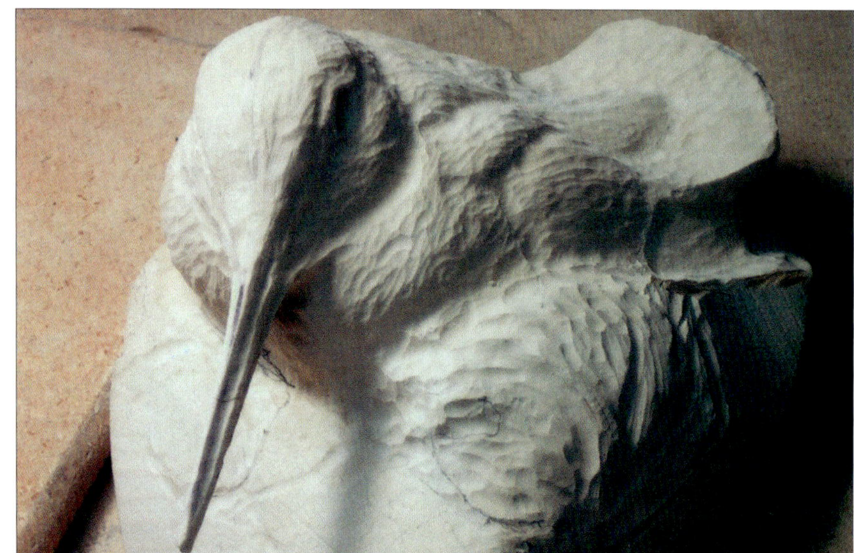

12 Refer to a study bill to mark and carve the nostrils at the base of the bill. The nostrils are located on the center of the bill's ridge next to the forehead. Use a 3-millimeter pointed diamond to carve the tiny oval opening of the nostril and the small lid above the opening. When you are finished seal the bill with CA glue.

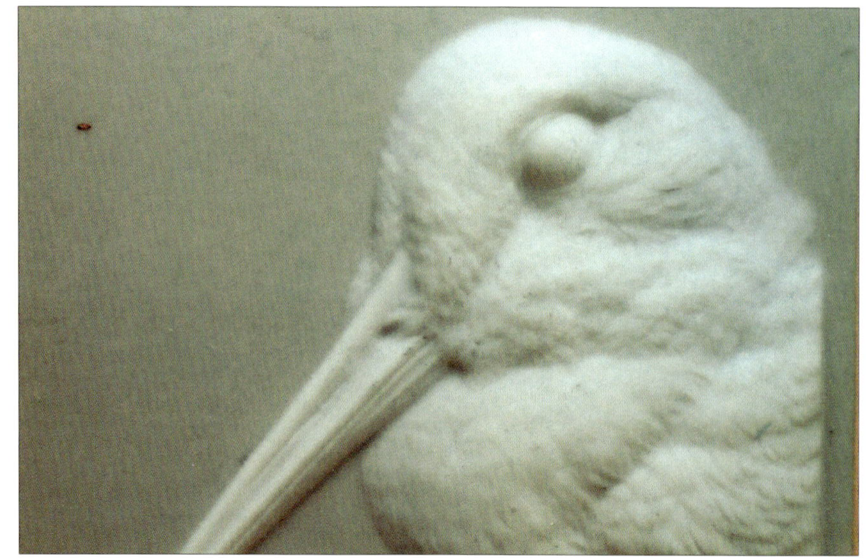

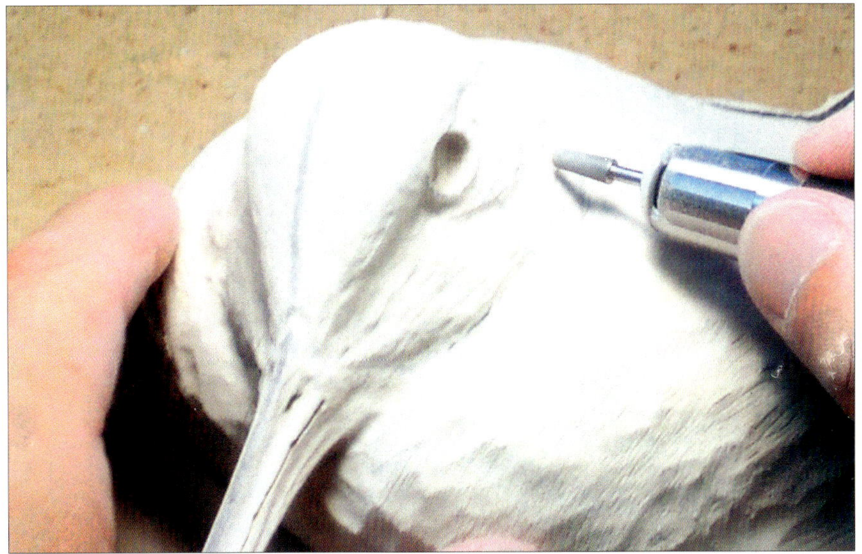

13 Contour the side of the head with a 4-millimeter diamond bullet so it blends into the body. Notice how the eye channel extends from the bill through the eye.

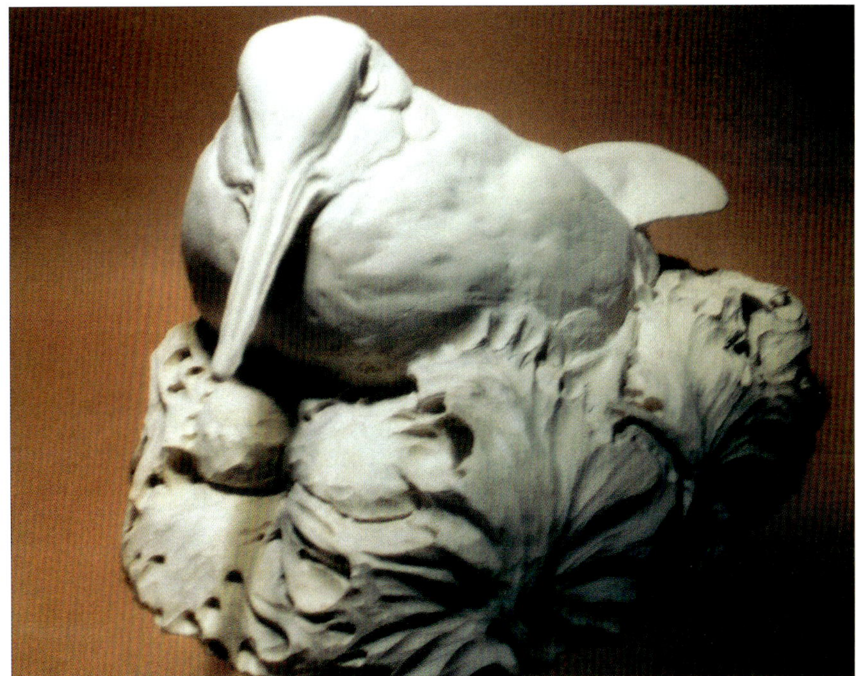

14 Once you are satisfied with the overall shape and attitude of the bird, sand it down and you are ready for eye placement and feathering. As you can see, I also added habitat beneath my woodcock. Rocks, moss, and leaves are abundant where all three birds in this book are located. A rock can be almost any shape you choose, so long as it fits pleasantly within your composition. I use both a flat-edge stump-cutter and a round stump-cutter to shape the rocks, and a thin, tapered diamond bit to form the crevices between rocks. I make indentations in the rocks with the tip of a bullet diamond cutter and paint them with a wash of Jo Sonja's Burnt Umber and Liquitex Ultramarine Blue.

I create moss in my carvings with a moss-cutter, which is simply a thin, tapered diamond bit available from Jaymes Company in Forest Hill, Maryland. Hundreds of holes are poked in the wood and then connected with the same bit. I then color the moss with separate applications of Jo Sonja's Yellow and Moss Green.

As far as the leaves are concerned, I simply pencil them on in a pleasing pattern. Then I remove wood on the outside of each leaf, create a concave depression inside the leaf with a diamond bullet or stump-cutter, and carve veins with a small diamond bit. Finally, I paint the leaves the color of species I have chosen (for example, oak, maple, birch, etc.). The main thing to consider when creating habitat in bird carvings is what effect it will have within the composition as a whole. If you let your creative talents wander you will be surprised at what you can accomplish. Sometimes the shape of the wood will tell you what to do.

15 I have developed a system for eye-setting that does not require putty. I used this same procedure on all three of the birds in this book, and will demonstrate on a flat carving of a woodcock. The first step is to establish the eye position as you did earlier.

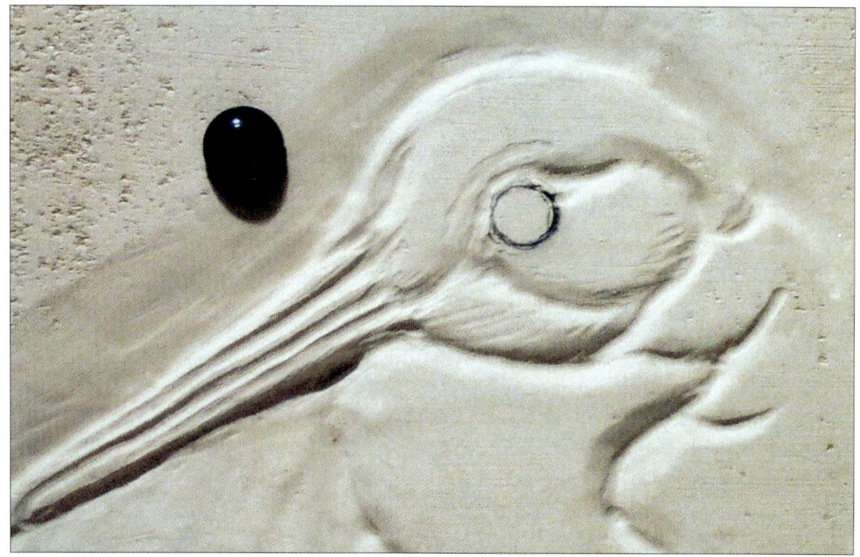

16 Then carve the 3-millimeter-deep, 9-millimeter-wide depression with a 3- or 4-millimeter diamond bullet as shown.

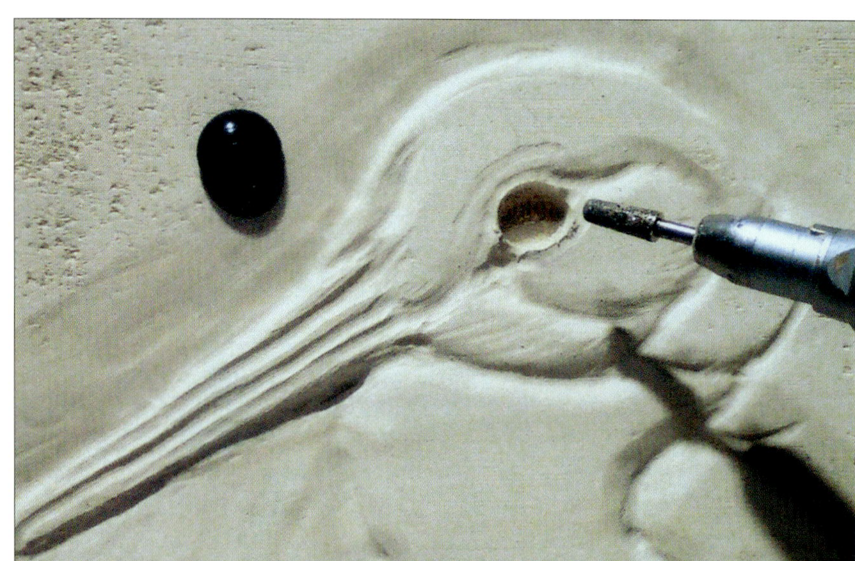

17 Undercut the upper lid to a depth of approximately 4 millimeters with a 3-millimeter diamond ball. Cut the lower lid to a depth of 2 millimeters.

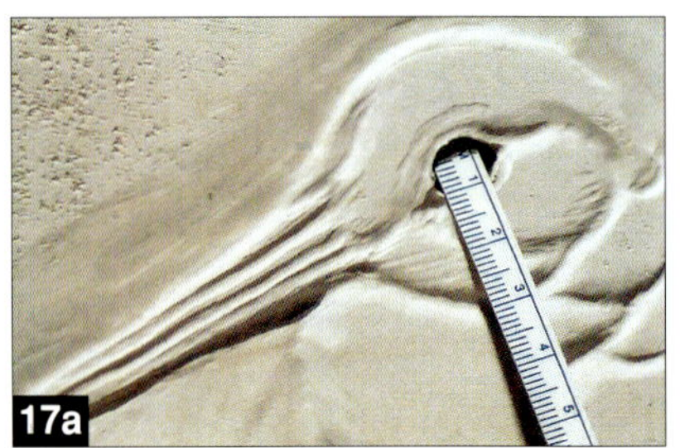

17a

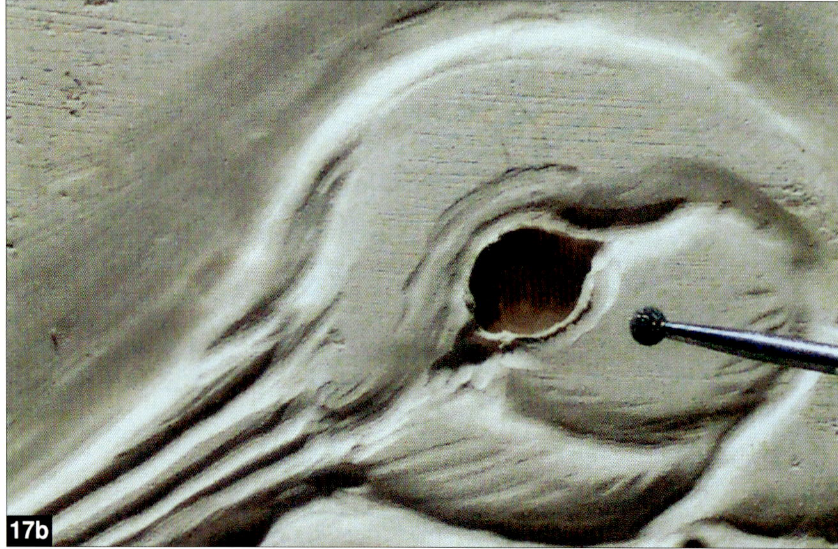

17b

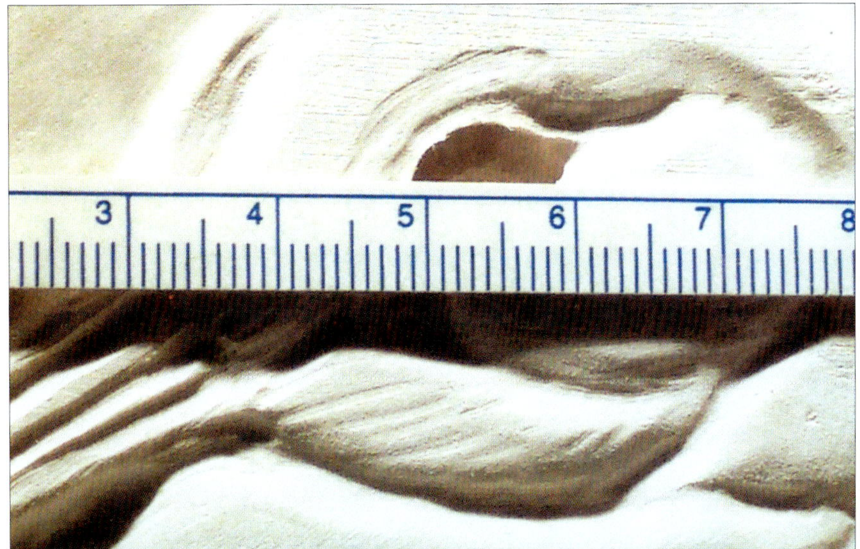

18 The eye cavity is now 9 millimeters wide to accept the 10-millimeter eye.

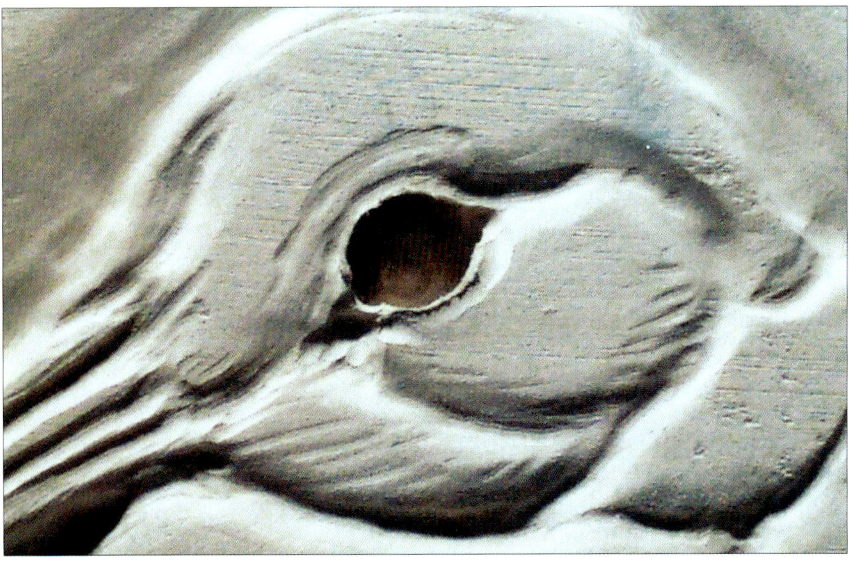

19 At this point the eyehole is ready for the eye insertion.

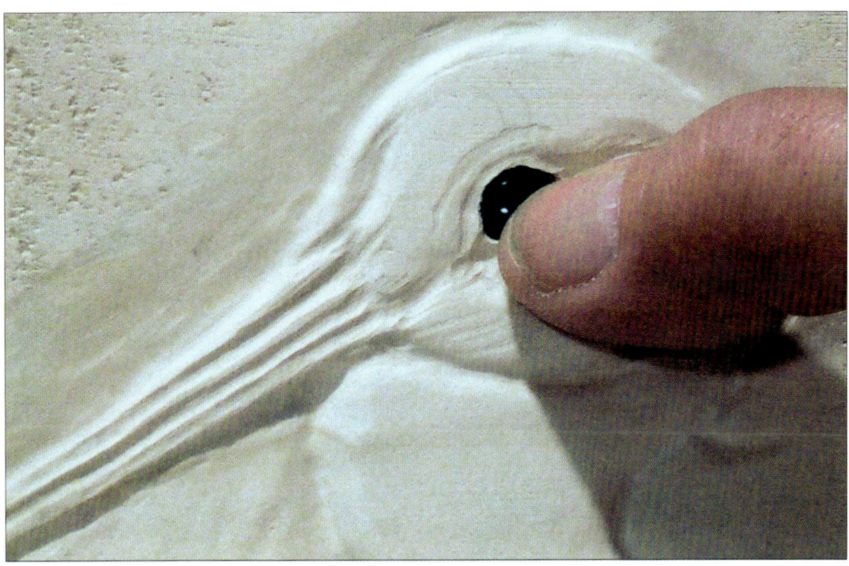

20 Simply press the eye into the socket with a finger or dowel. Minor adjustments may need to be made if the eye does not snap into place.

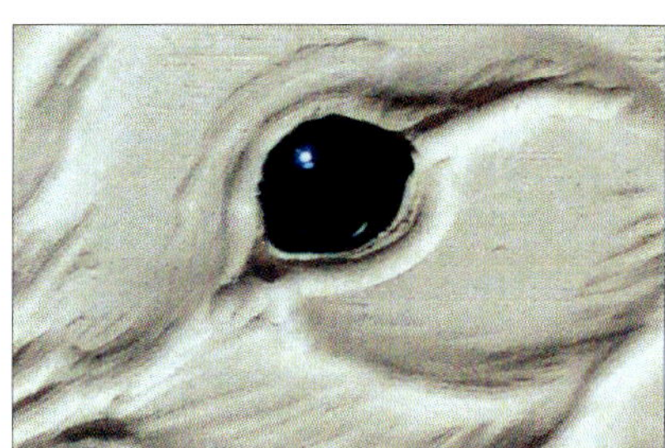

The eye is in place.

TEXTURING AND BURNING THE AMERICAN WOODCOCK

FIGURE 1

Seen here are all the different types of feathers you will find on an American woodcock. Use this figure as reference when texturing and burning your piece.

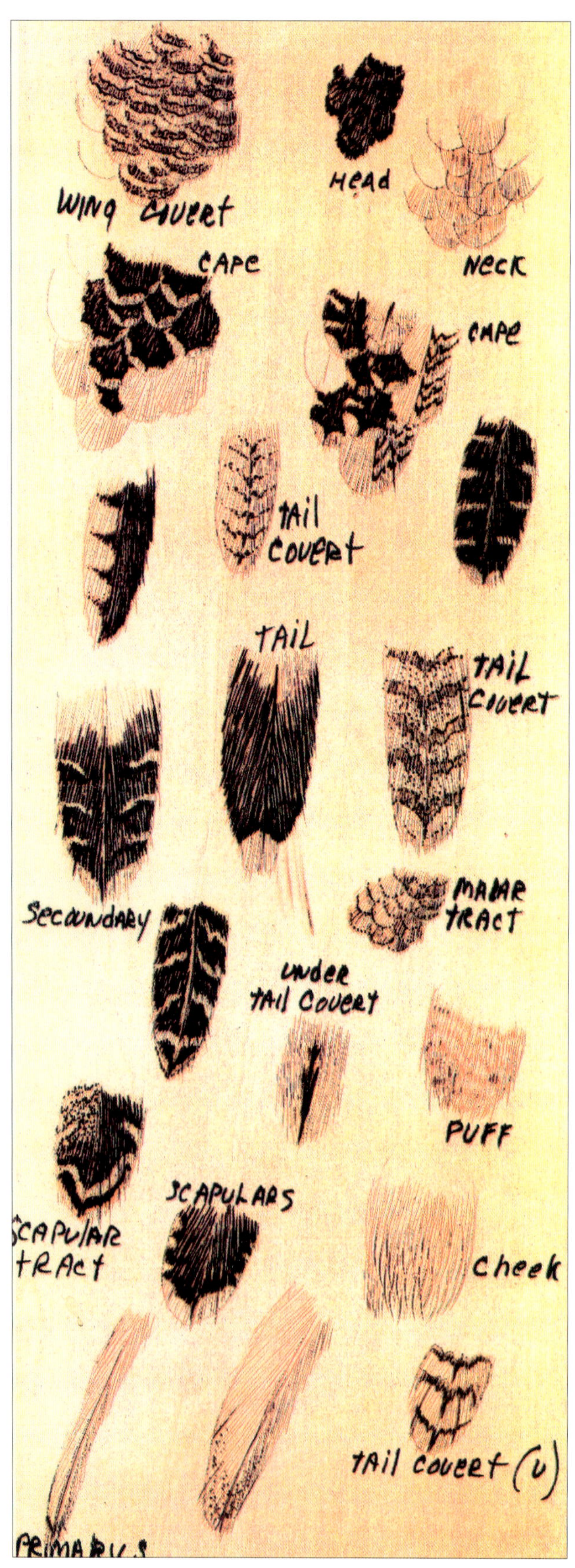

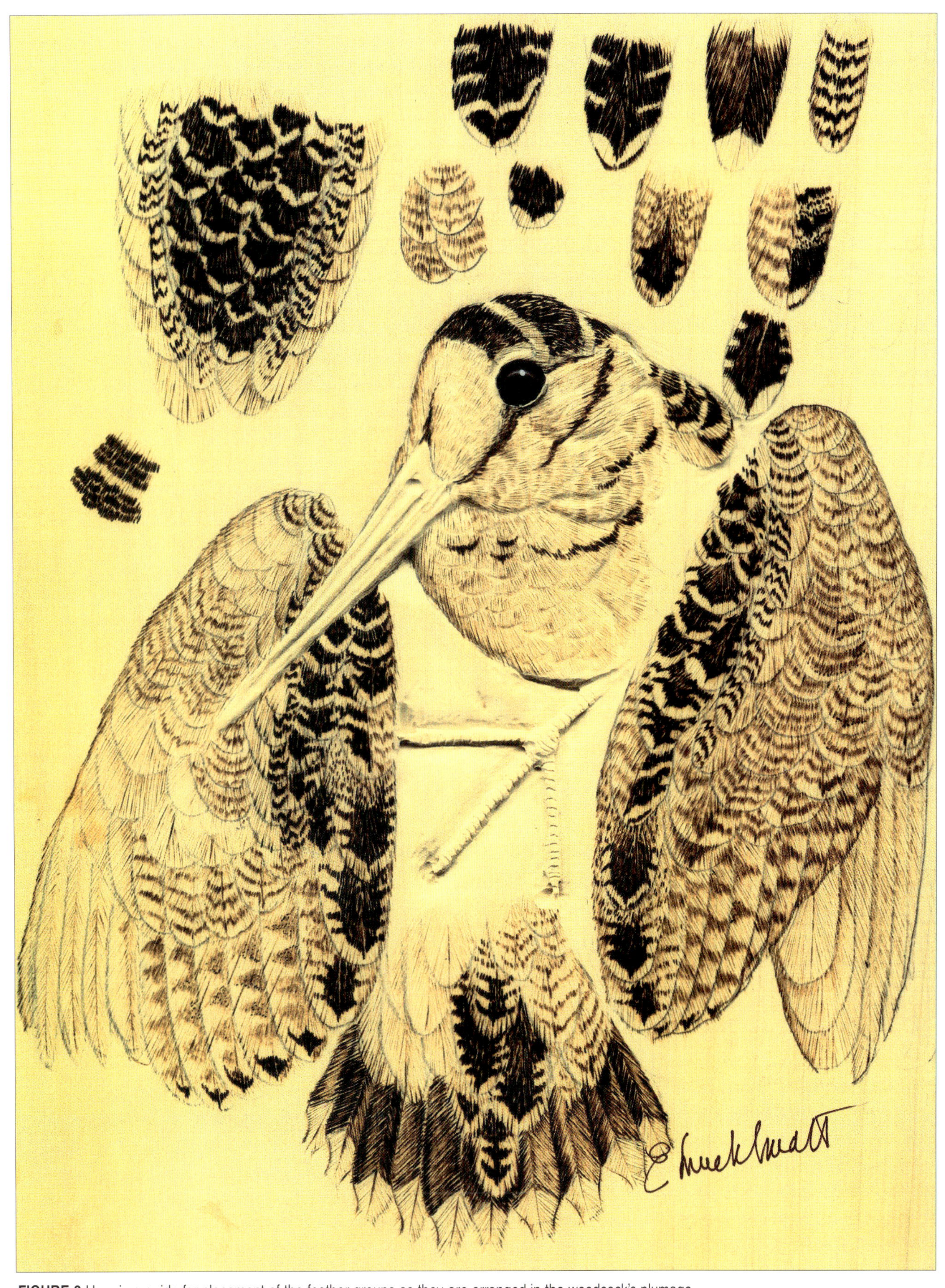

FIGURE 2 Here is a guide for placement of the feather groups as they are arranged in the woodcock's plumage.

FIGURE 3 I use a wide variety of burning tips on my birds. From left to right: feather-edger, blunt point, sharp point, heavy tight round, regular tight round, and sharp spear. I also use a blunt spear, which is not shown.

I use the feather-edger to raise the feather tips of the flight and tail feathers. The blunt-point and sharp-point tips work well for shaping feather barbs. The choice between the two lies with the individual carver; I have personally found that the sharp point has a tendency to dig in at the point of contact with the quill as you attempt to burn the lazy S-shaped barb.

The heavy and regular tight round tips are used where large sections of heavy burning are needed (for example, the three dark patches on the top of the woodcock's head).

The sharp and blunt spears can be used to separate the upper and lower mandibles of a bird's bill, to make small feathers around the forehead area, and to create the scales on top of the carved toes.

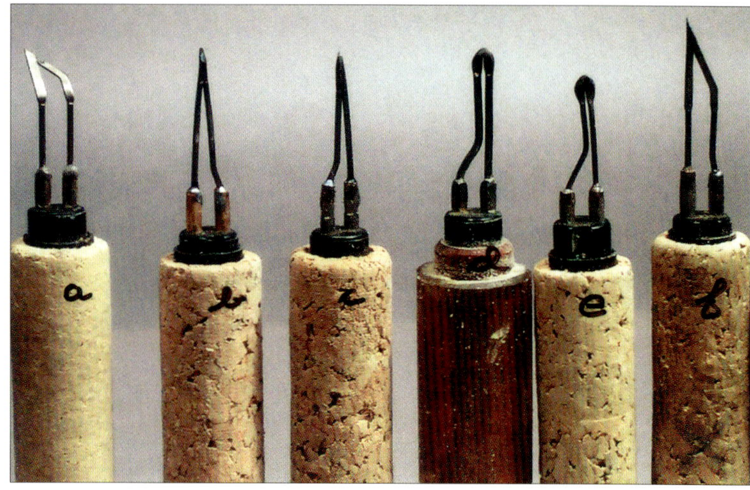

1 The first step in the texturing process is to draw the feather layout on your bird with a pencil.

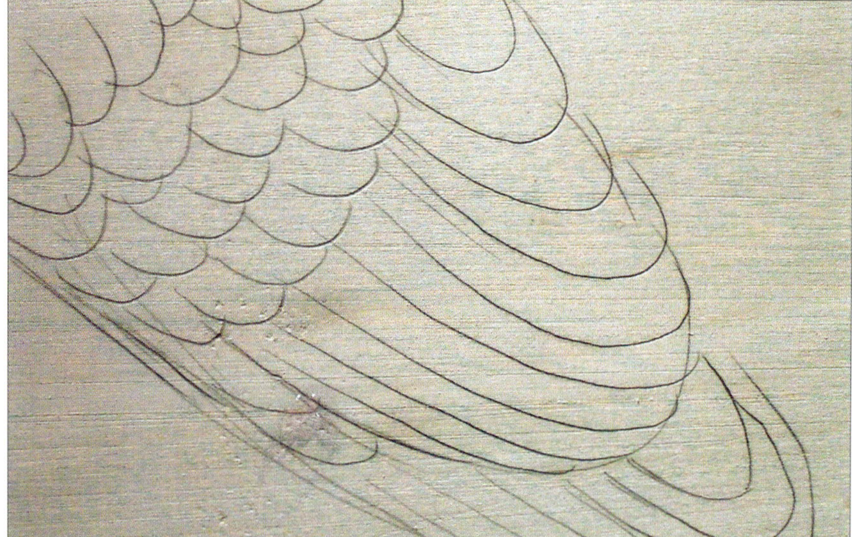

2 Then use a diamond ball to carve around each feather.

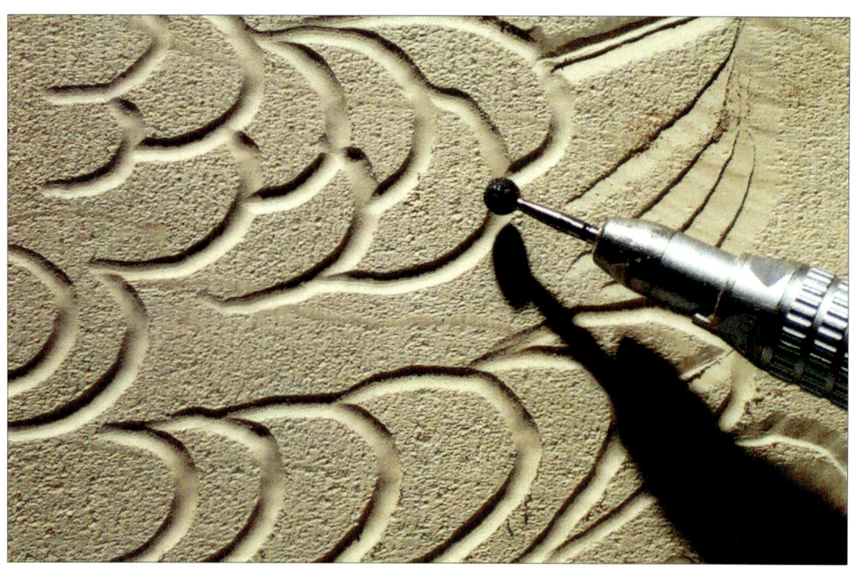

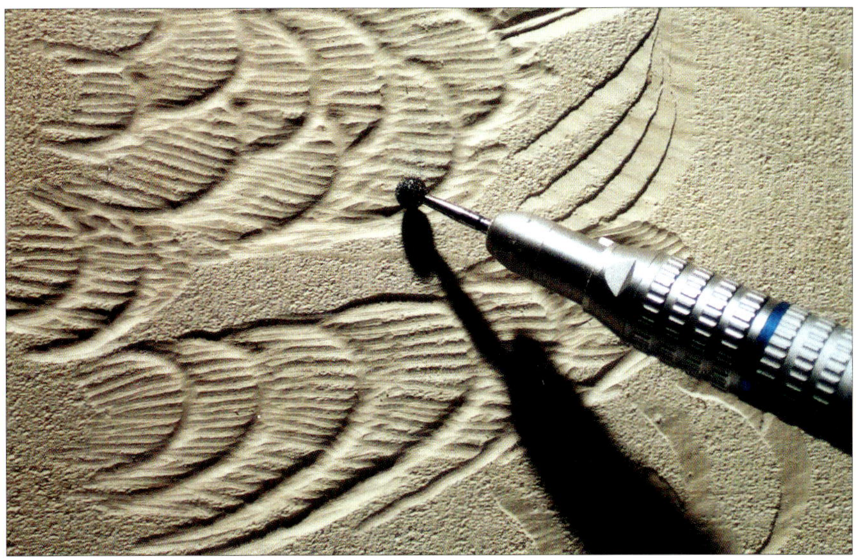

3 Round both the leading edges of the feathers and the area where one feather meets another.

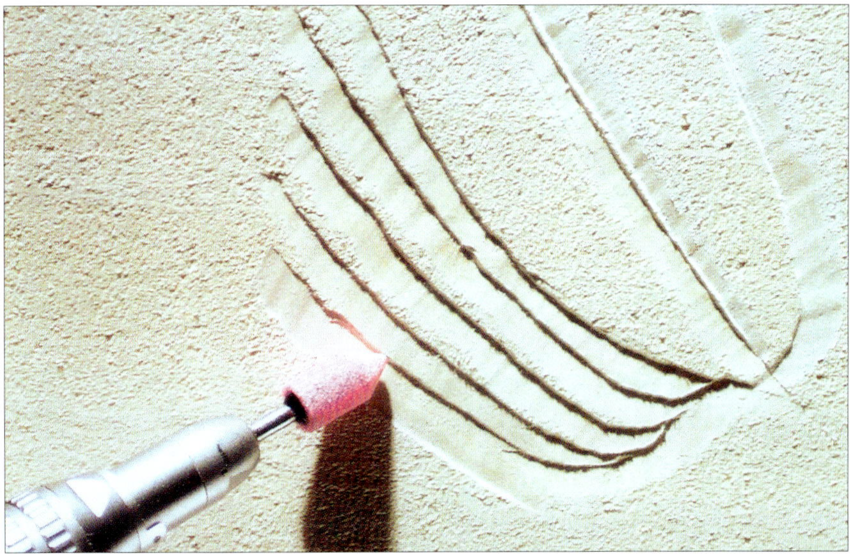

4 I carve the longer feathers with a tapered stone. Stones are sold in a variety of grits commonly designated by color. They increase in grit from white, to pink, to blue, to green. My general preference is for the white stone, though I am using a pink one here.

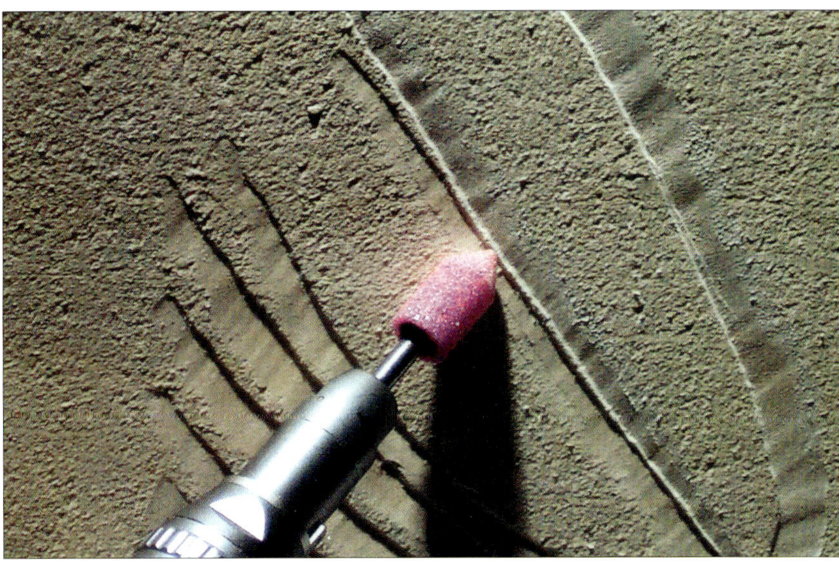

5 I use this same stone to shape the quills of the feathers. Draw two parallel lines along the center of the feather with a rotating tapered white stone (the high-speed micromotor will perform best at half rpm's—it's easier to control when run at half-speed.) These lines should converge at the tip of the feather.

6 This photo shows all of the wing feathers carved out.

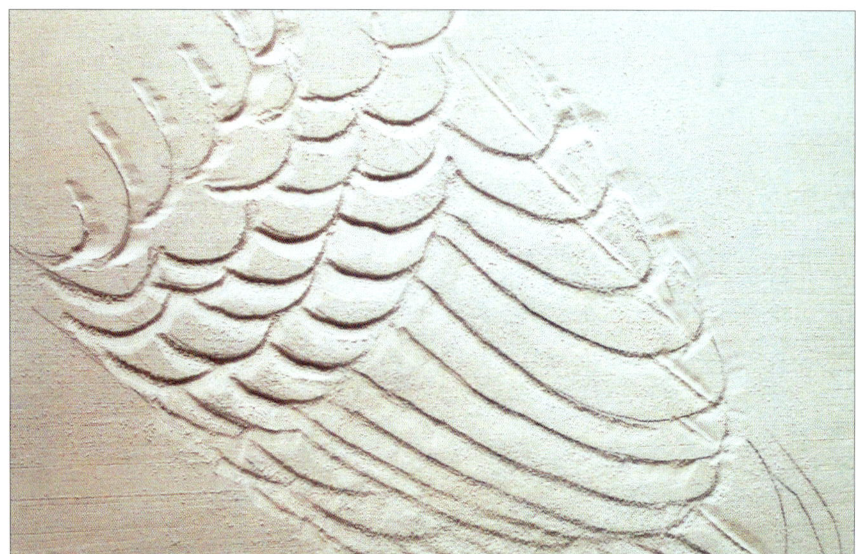

7 The correct technique when you begin stoning feathers is to hold the handpiece loosely between the thumb and forefinger away from the tip.

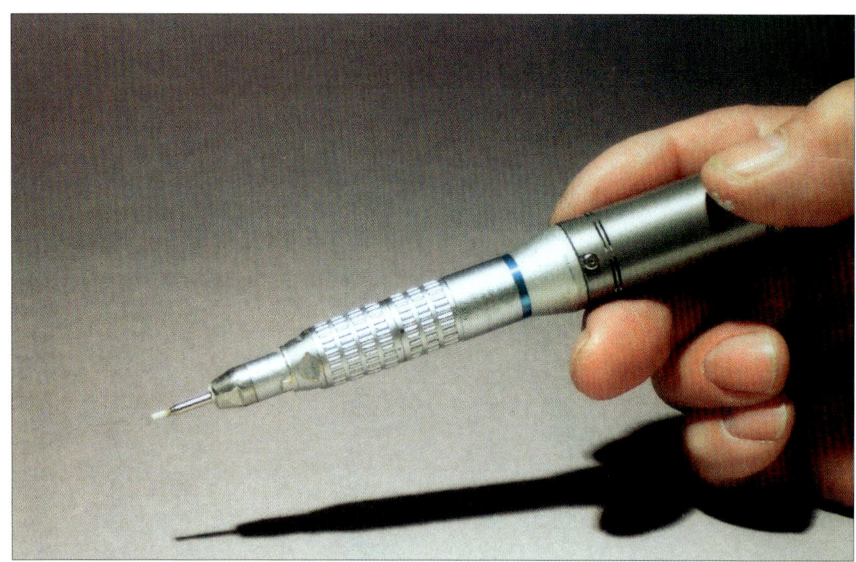

8 When you have your wing feathers delineated, stone individual barbs into the feathers with a white straight-edged stone.

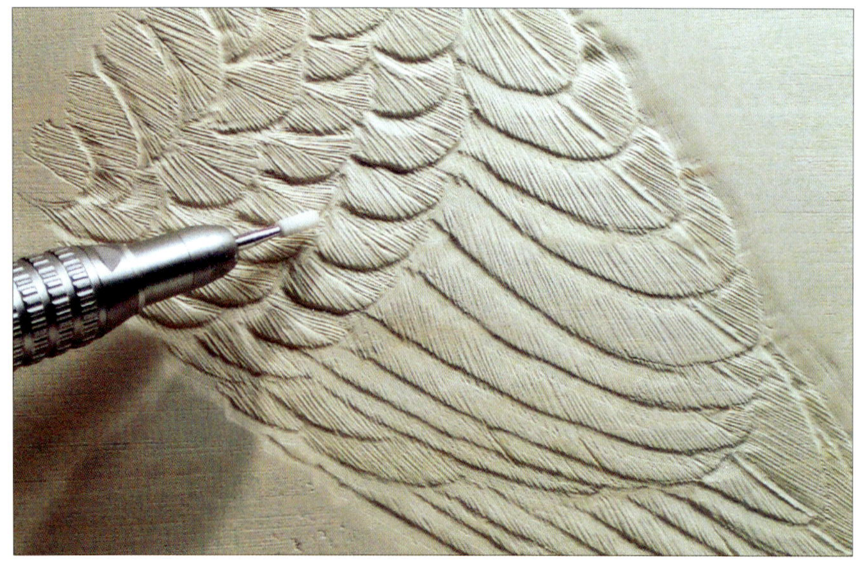

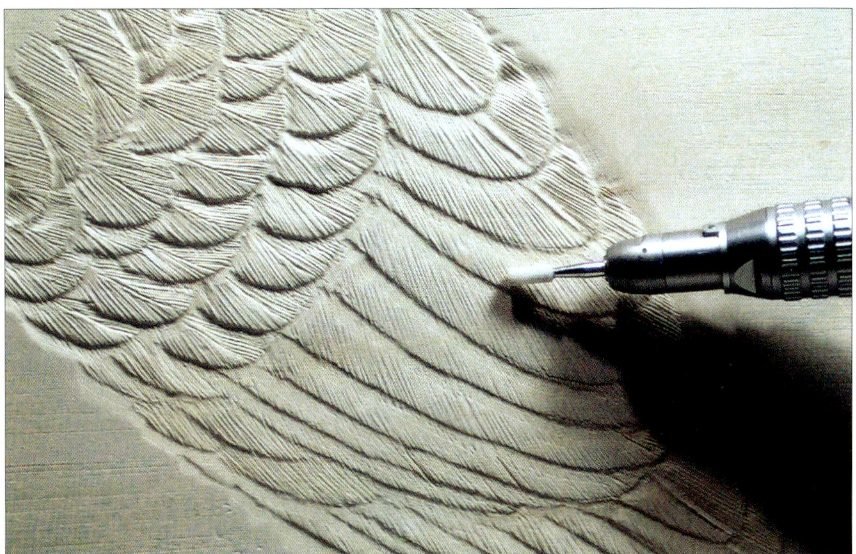

9 Stone the individual barbs downward from the quill to the feather's leading edge.

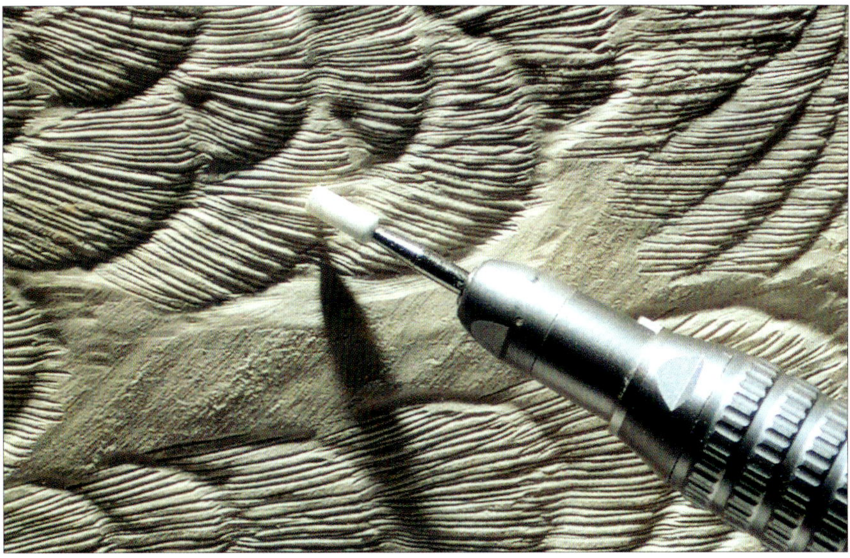

10 This photo shows the stoning of the wing magnified two times.

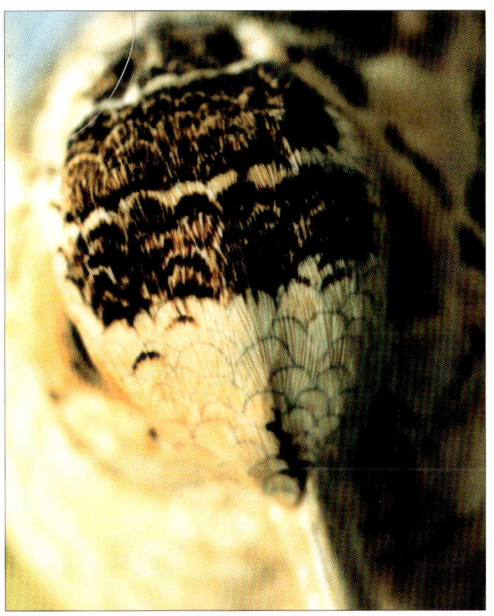

11 When you are satisfied with your stoning, burn three dark bands of feathers on the crest of the woodcock's head. Three thin, light bands separate the burned bands.

12 Burn the feathers of the head, body, and tail as seen here, referring to Figures 1 and 2 as guides to specific feather regions.

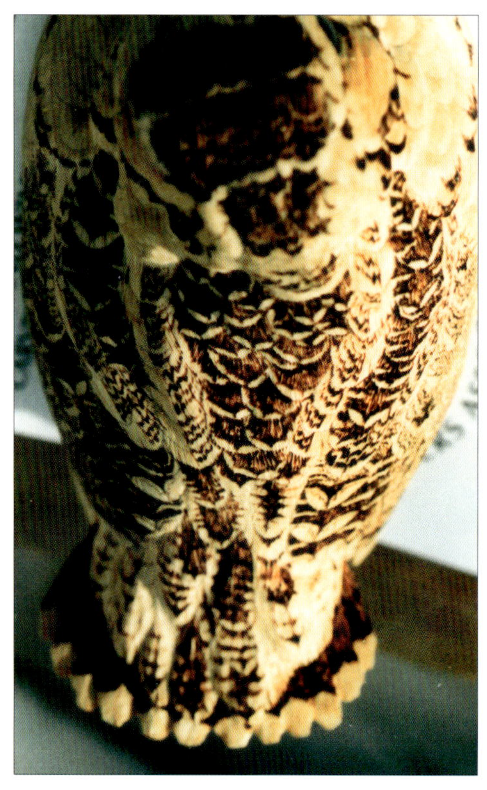

13 Burn the scapulars and coverts as shown. Be sure to maintain a consistent heat-level within each section of your carving.

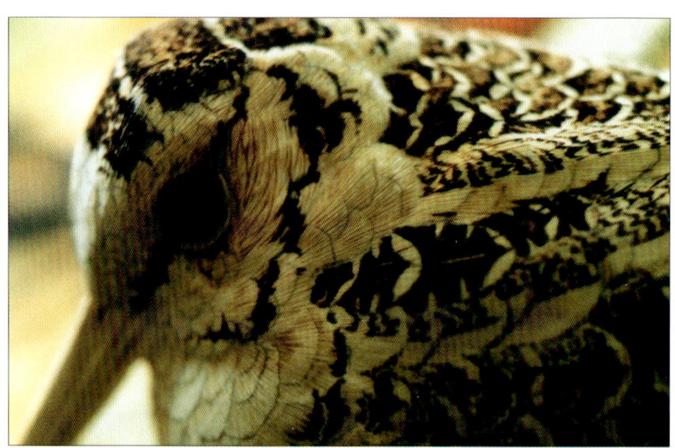

14 In this photo the head, cape, scapulars, and coverts have been burned completely. Use a light burning-touch on the sides of the head into the chest area.

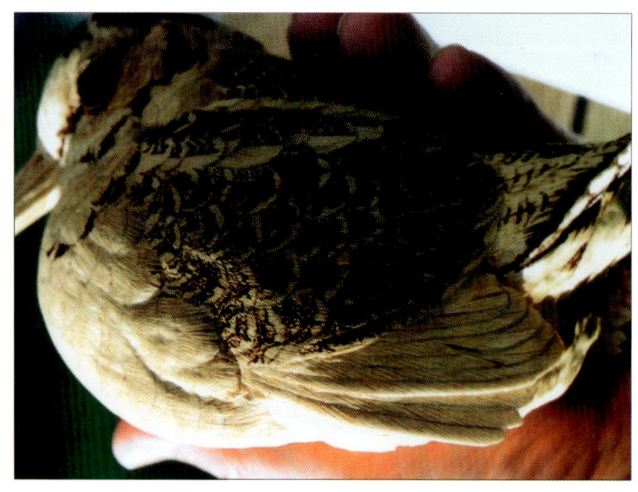

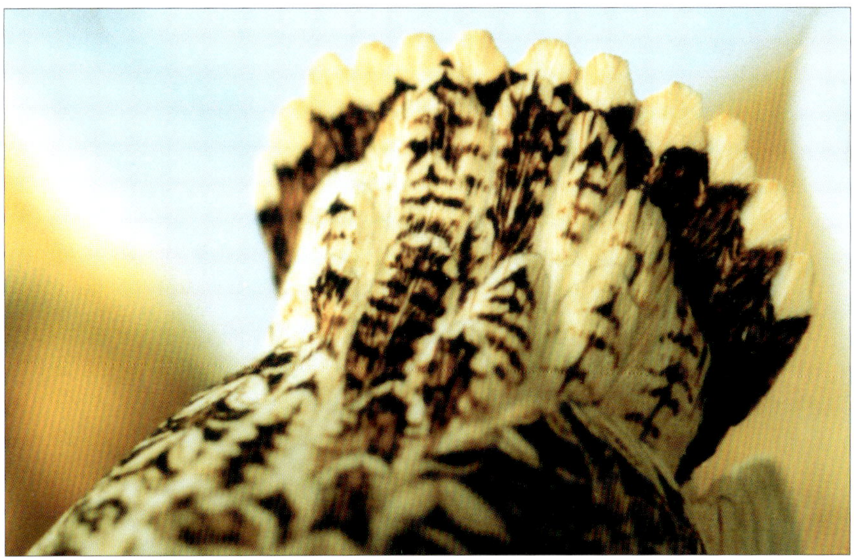

15 Burn the tail feathers and tail coverts as shown here.

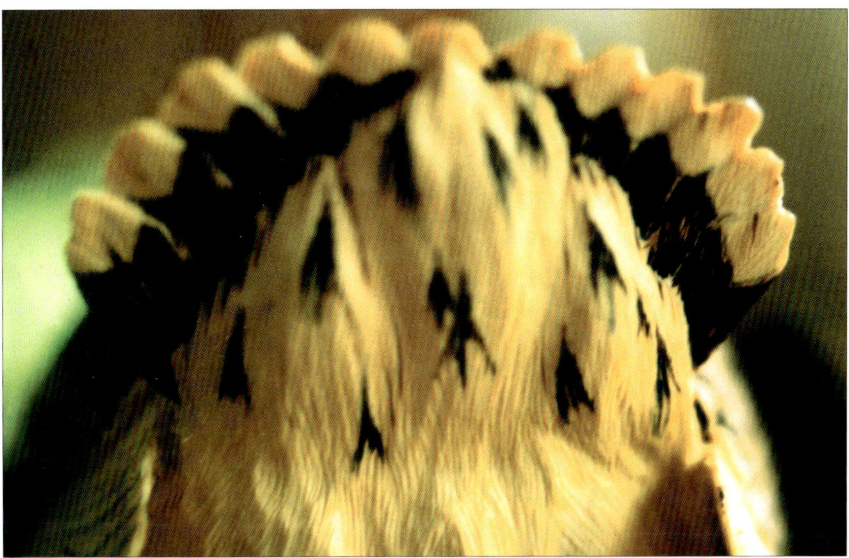

16 Here is a shot of the burning on the underside of the tail.

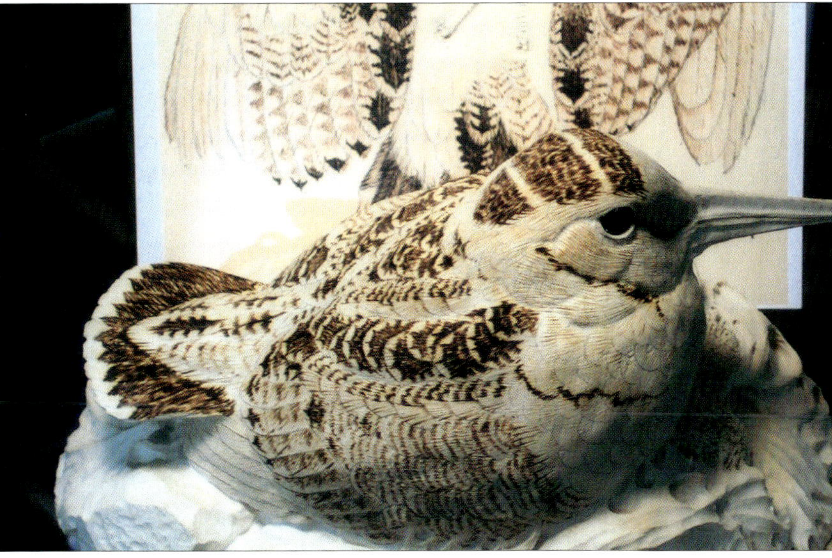

17 All of the woodcock's feather groups have been burned.

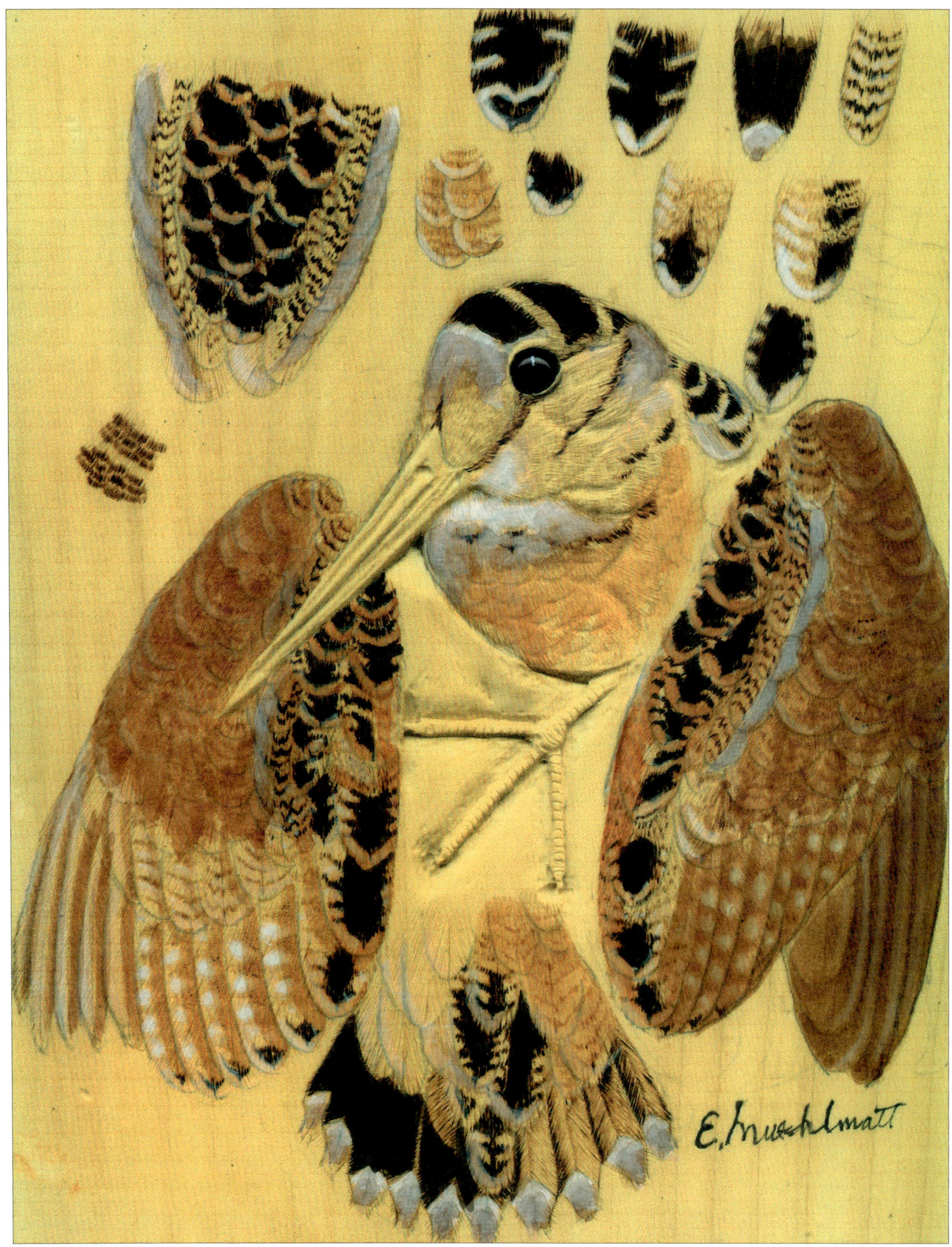

FIGURE 1 These are what the feather groups of the woodcock should look like when completely painted.

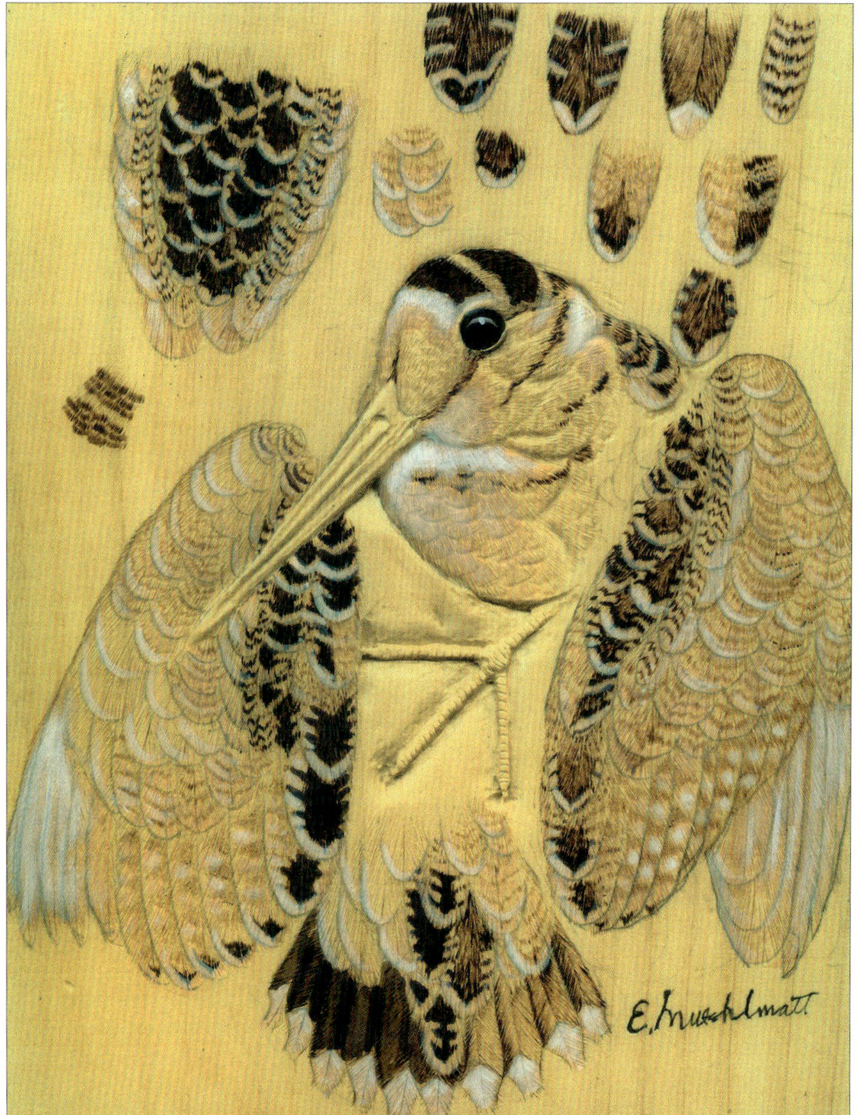

FIGURE 2 Use gesso mixed 50/50 with water to paint the following areas of the bird as shown here: the back of the neck, the upper forehead, the upper eye area, the front part of the cheeks, the bib, the primaries, the light areas of the cape, the upper-wing coverts, the light areas of the secondaries, the tail tips on the top and undersides, and the feather edges on the rump (both top and undersides).

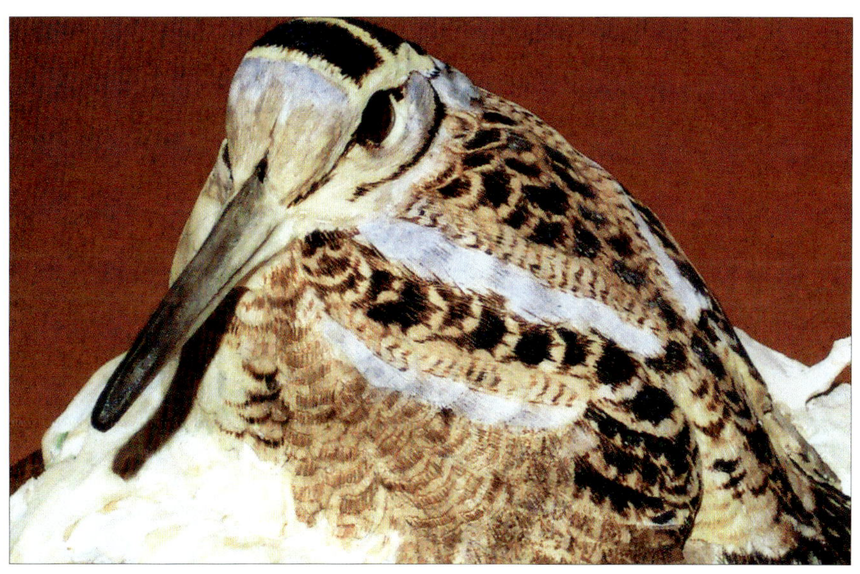

1 Mix up a gray wash out of Ultramarine Blue and Burnt Sienna. This color is applied in various shades to the feathers on the cape and upper secondaries, the upper forehead, the back of the neck, the rear part of the cheeks and around the white bib area, the tips of the rump feathers, the top of the tail, and on some of the lower-wing coverts. Some feathers should have a light and a dark side, separated by the quill.

2 With a wash of Burnt Umber, paint the primaries and the light-barred areas of the secondaries. Stipple some of this color on the upper-wing coverts as well.

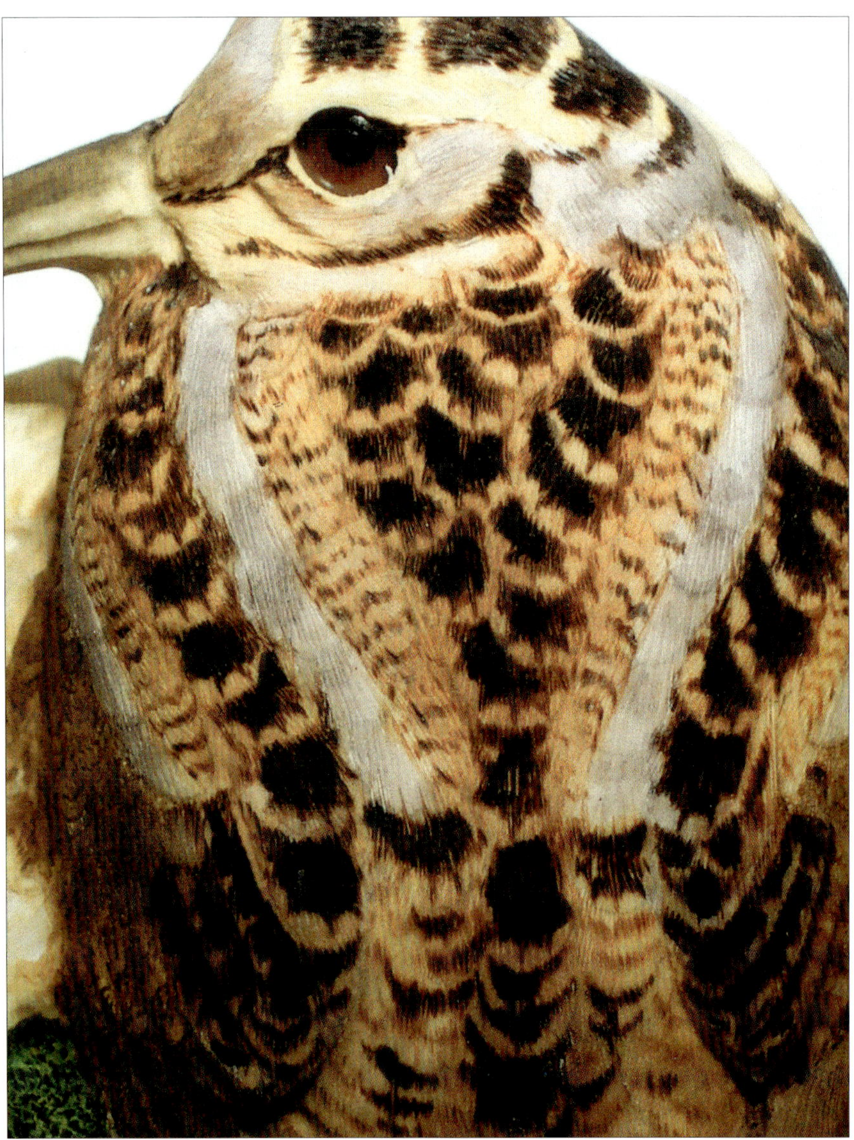

3 Mix three separate washes: one of Burnt Sienna, one of Bronze Yellow, and one of Raw Umber. Use these to paint the side of the breast, the flanks, the underside of the rear, and all the lightly burned areas on the wings, back, and rump. The Bronze Yellow wash is applied to the side of the breast and all of the lightly burned areas on the wings, back, and rump. Apply the Burnt Sienna wash to the flanks and the Raw Umber wash to the underside of the rear.

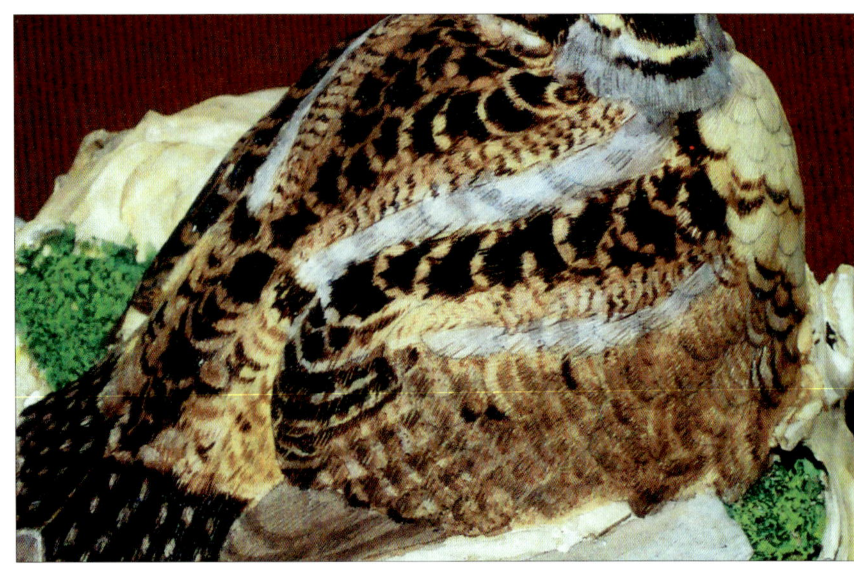

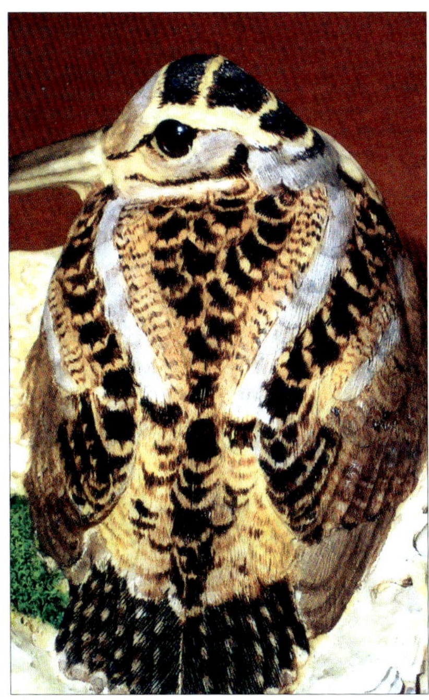

4 Use a wash of Burnt Umber to paint all of the deep brown areas of the wings and rump.

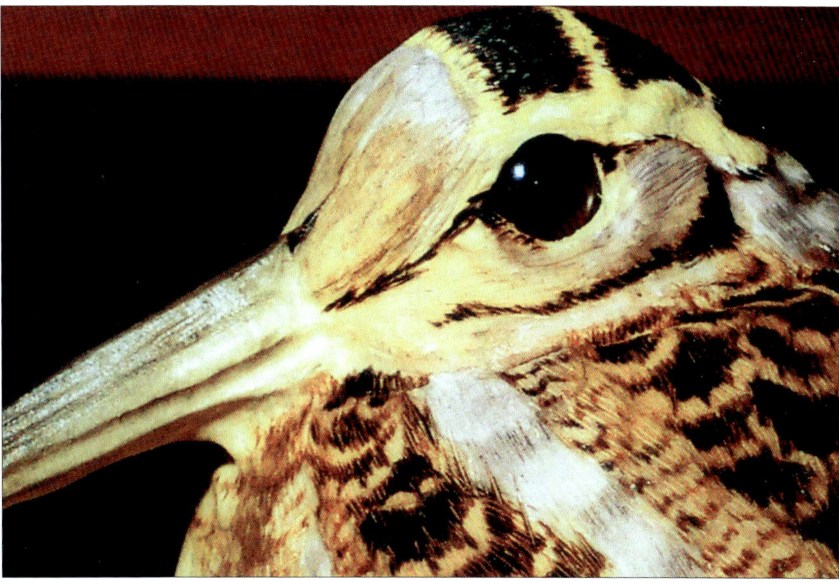

5 Using a wash of Raw Umber, paint the brown areas on the back of the neck, the cheeks, the upper chest, and the lower forehead. Then thin the wash even further and paint all the lightly burned areas on the wings, back, and rump. Use a strong wash of Warm Black to paint all the darkly burned areas on the bird. It's best if you have a photo of the bird to compare so that you can easily decipher what shade of brown gets painted in which area.

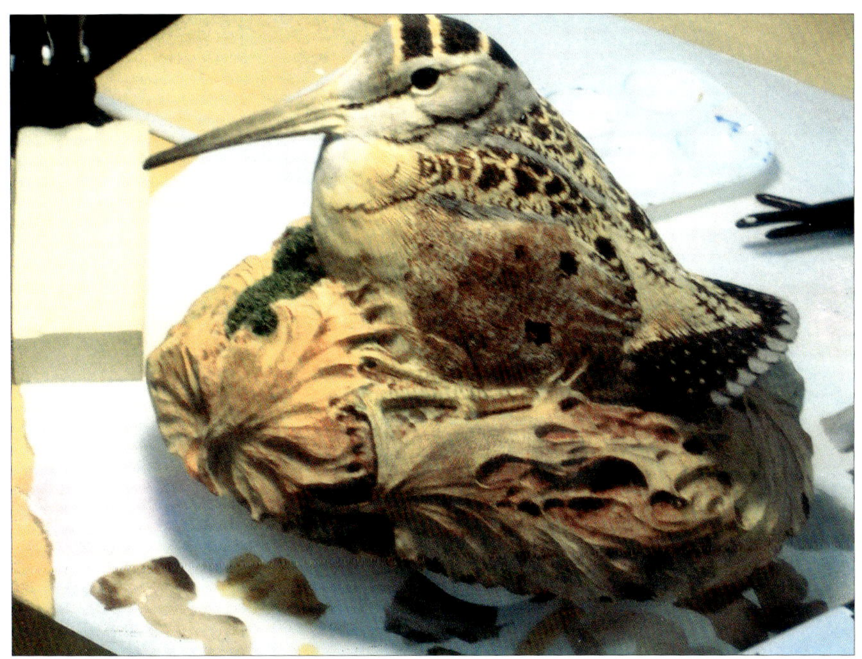

6 To tie everything together, wash the back, the wings, and the top of the rump with a mix of Ultramarine Blue and Burnt Umber. The amount of each color added to this mix is determined by the carver. The more Ultramarine Blue you use, the more gray you will get—the more Burnt Umber, the more brown. Add plenty of water; this should be a very light wash. Finally, use a strong Bronze Yellow wash to touch up the lightly burned bands on the top of the head, the narrow strips between the wide black areas, some of the lightly burned upper secondaries, and some of the rump feathers.

THE BOBWHITE QUAIL

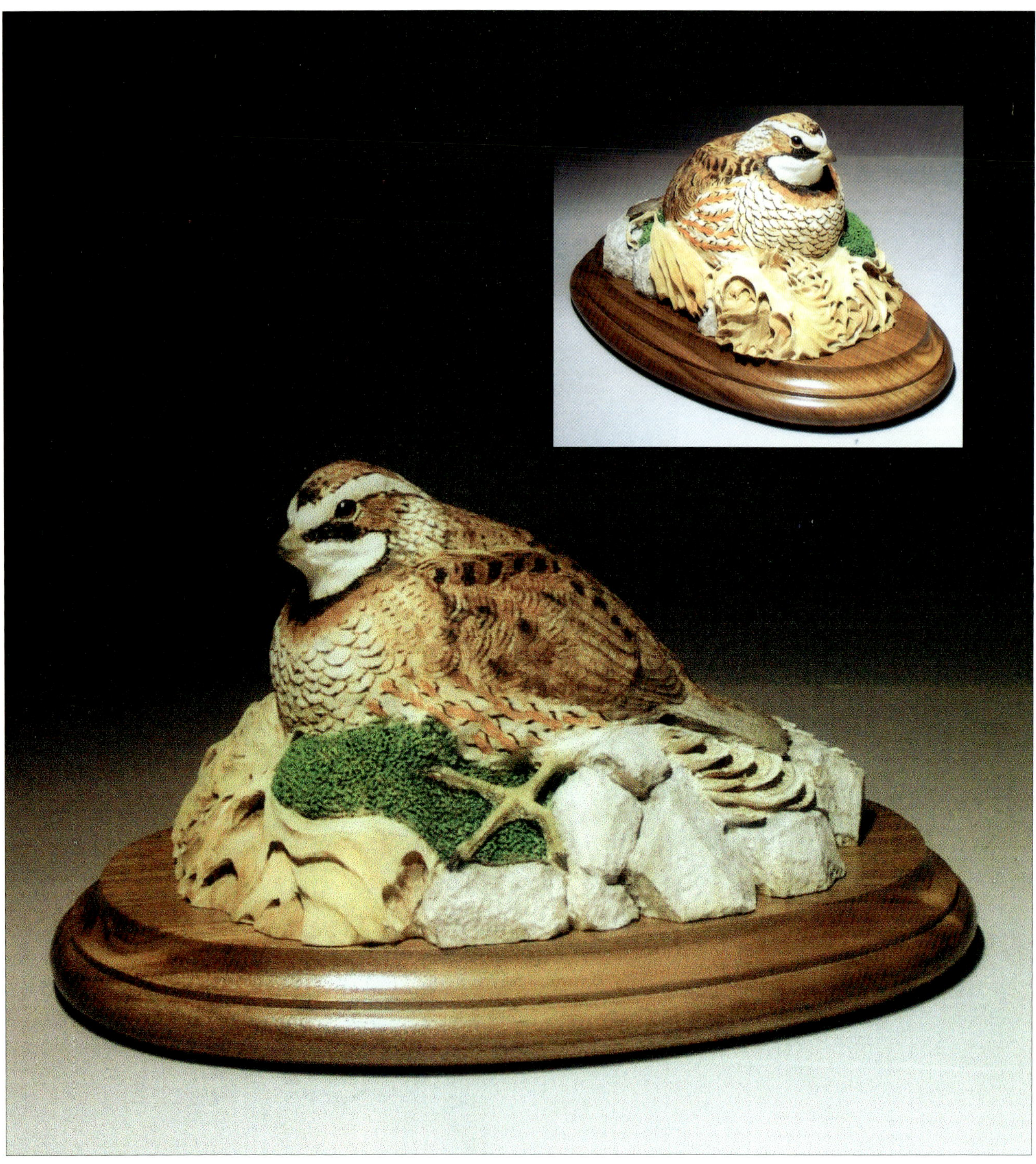

The next bird we will tackle is the bobwhite quail. Bobwhites measure from 9 to 11 inches in length and are common in the eastern and central United States. Unlike the third bird featured in this book, the ruffed grouse, bobwhite quails are not winter-hardy, and many of them die during the severe northern winters. To offset this condition, females often produce more than 20 hatchlings to a clutch. Both sexes of bobwhites gather in coveys, sometimes numbering more than 25 birds, and they tend to roost in a ring with their heads facing outward. For this bird you will need a 6- x 5- x 8-inch block of tupelo or other carving wood and a set of 8-millimeter brown glass eyes.

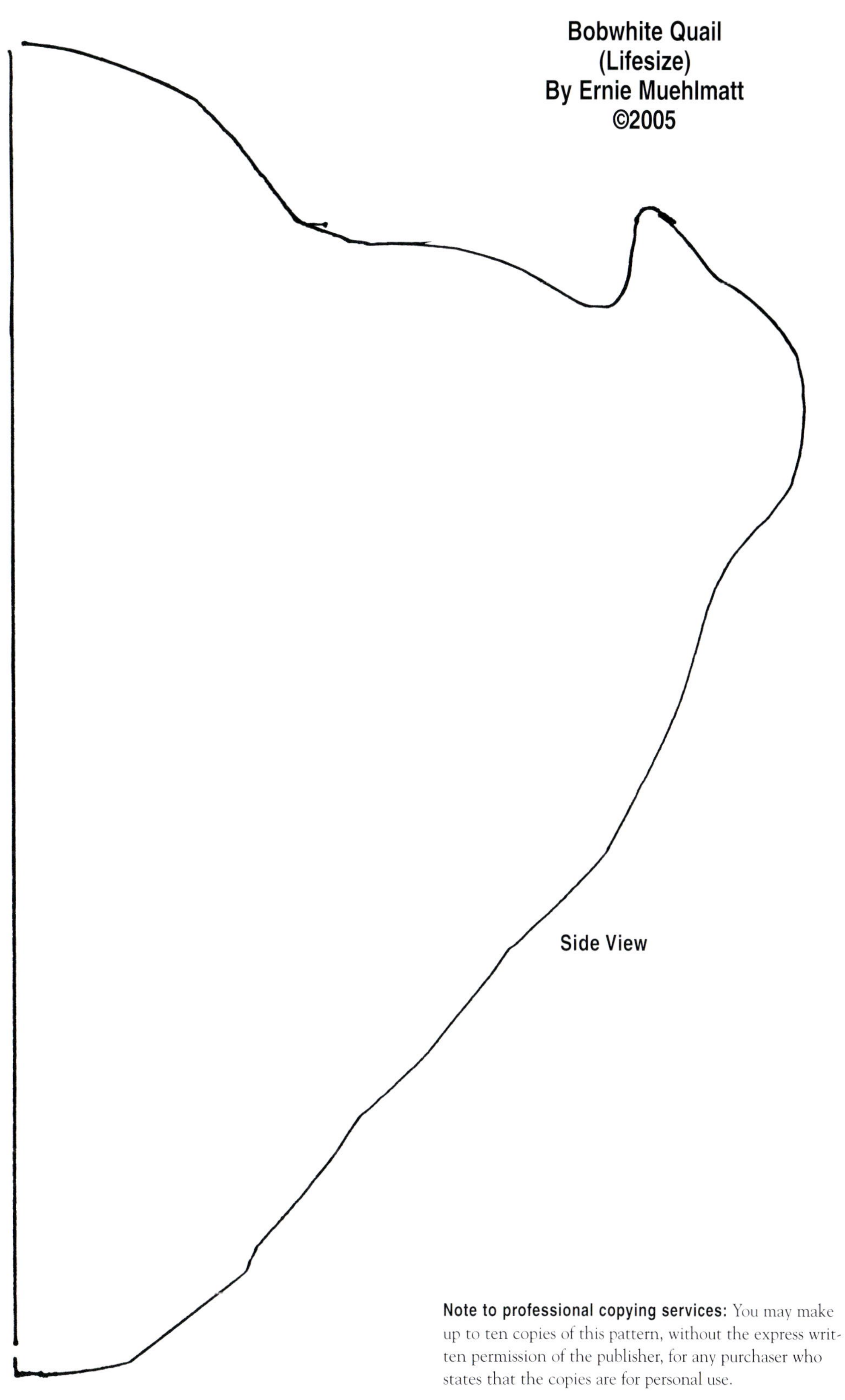

Note to professional copying services: You may make up to ten copies of this pattern, without the express written permission of the publisher, for any purchaser who states that the copies are for personal use.

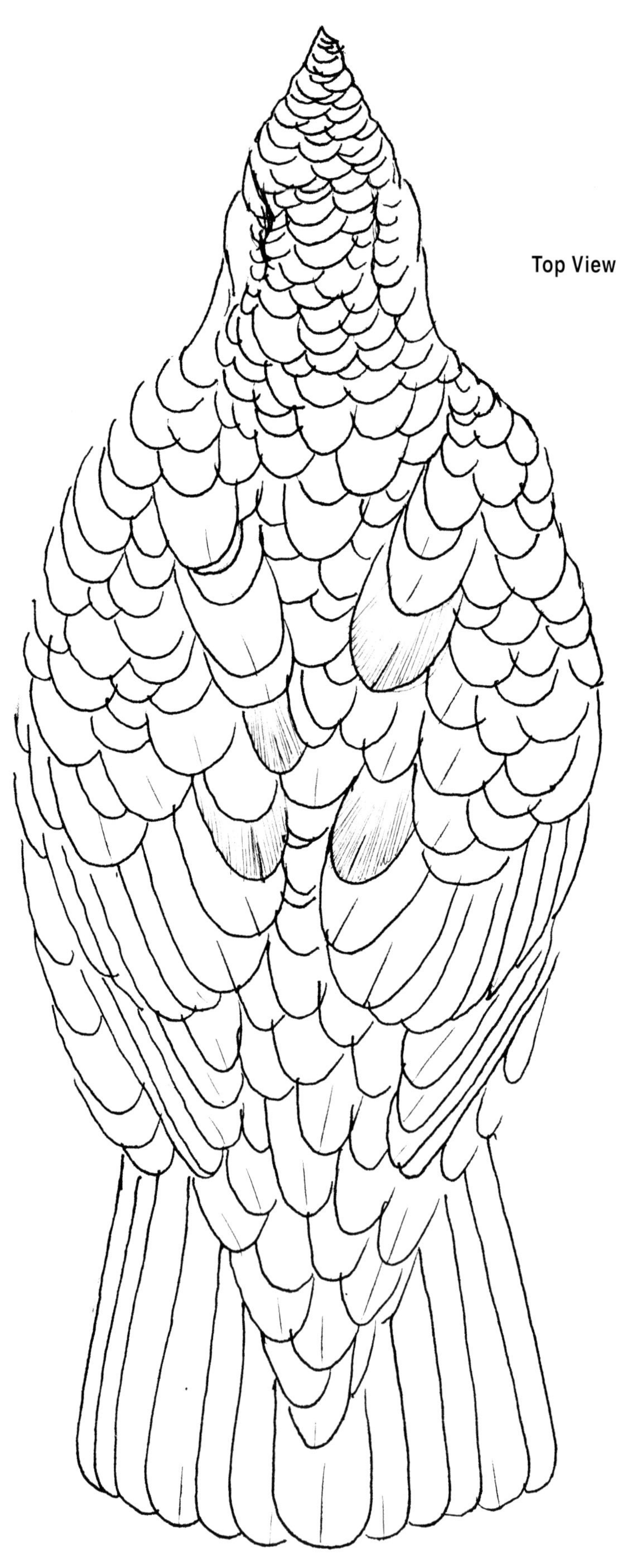
Top View

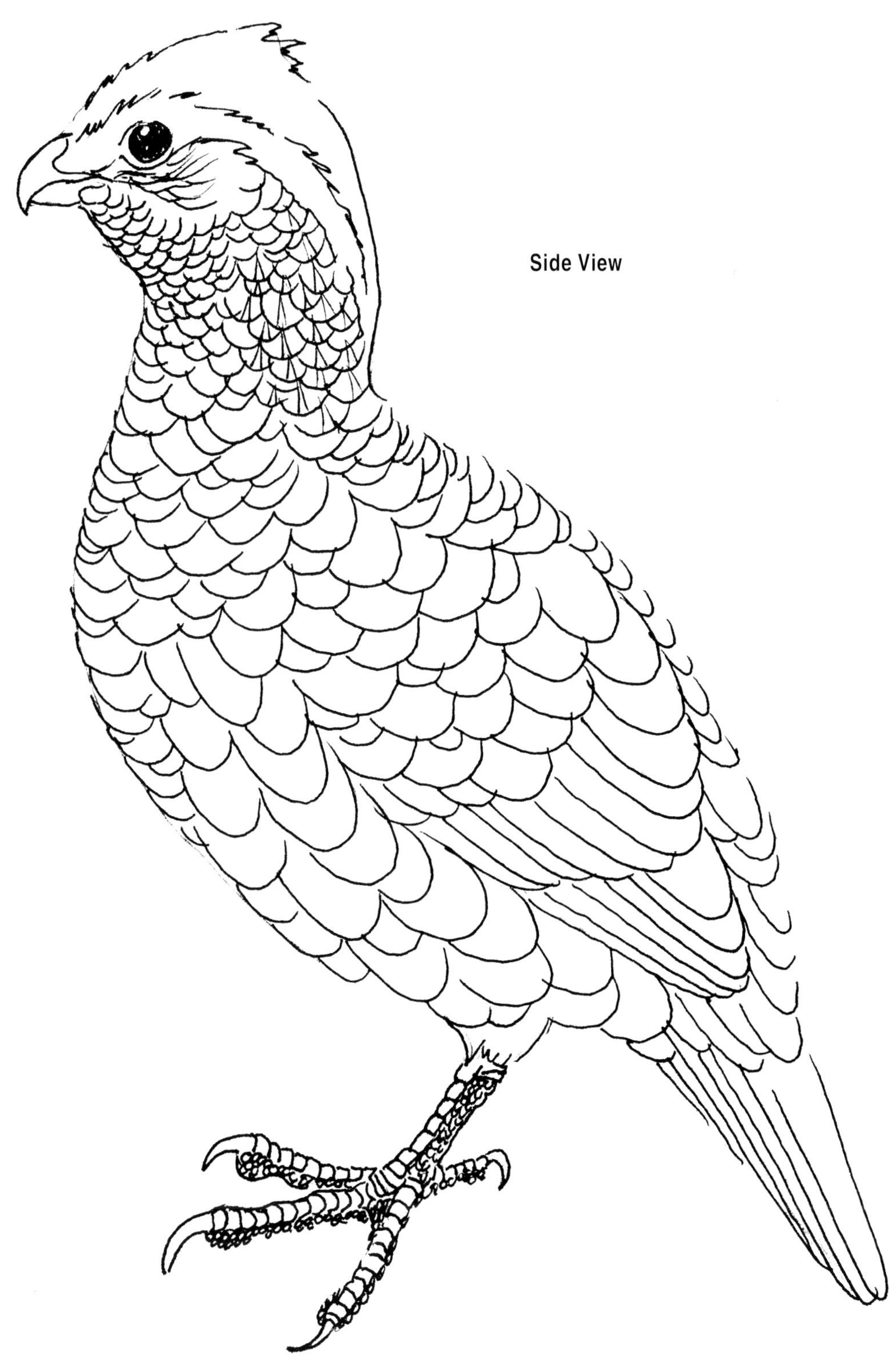
Side View

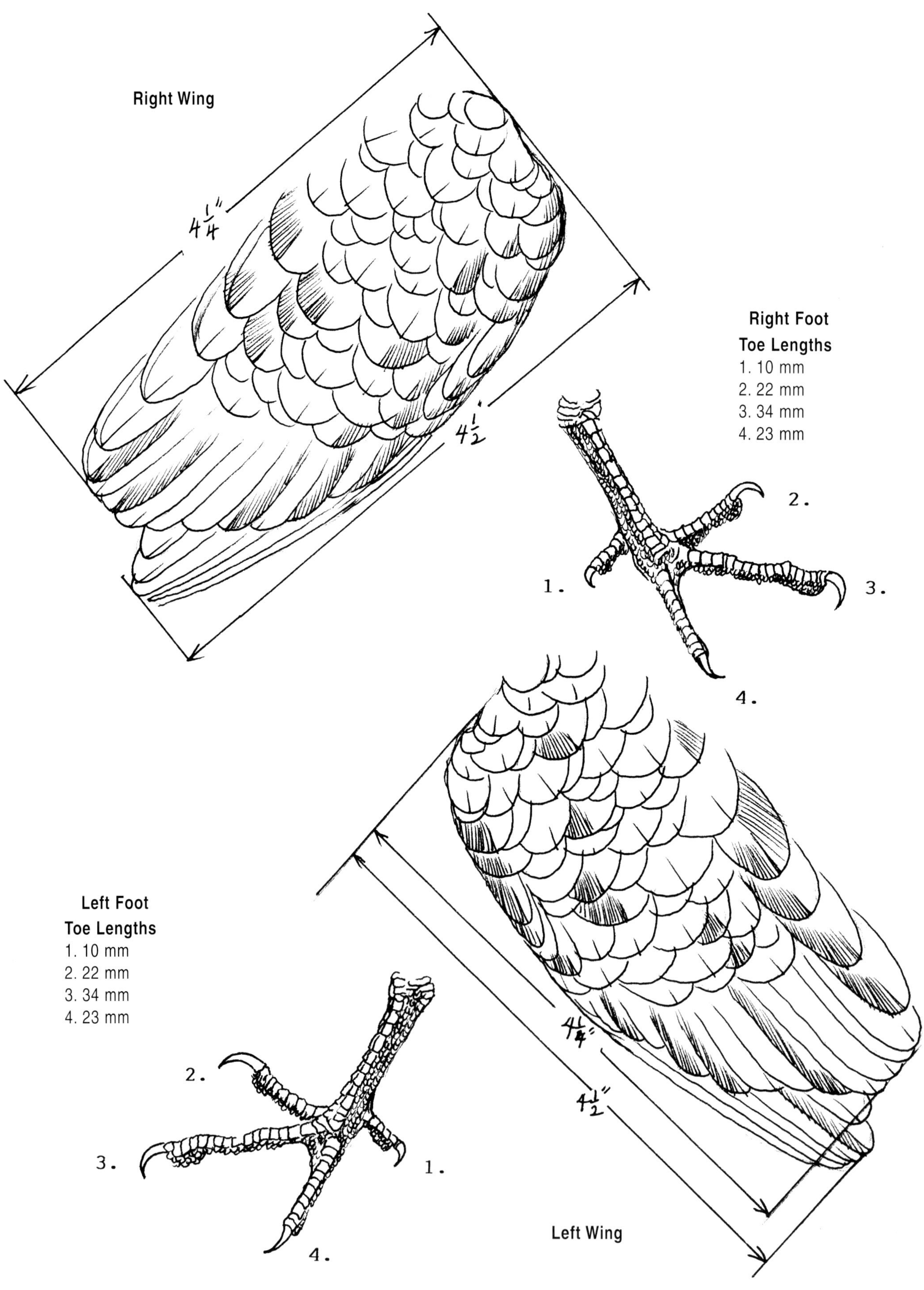
Right Wing
4 1/4"
4 1/2"
Right Foot
Toe Lengths
1. 10 mm
2. 22 mm
3. 34 mm
4. 23 mm
1.
2.
3.
4.
Left Foot
Toe Lengths
1. 10 mm
2. 22 mm
3. 34 mm
4. 23 mm
2.
3.
1.
4.
4 1/4"
4 1/2"
Left Wing

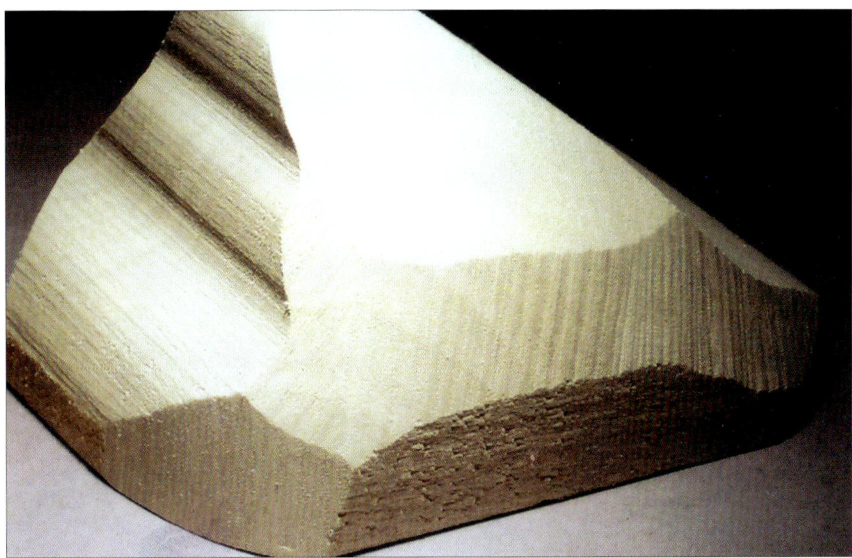

1 Here is the initial cutout I made on my band saw from the side and top view patterns.

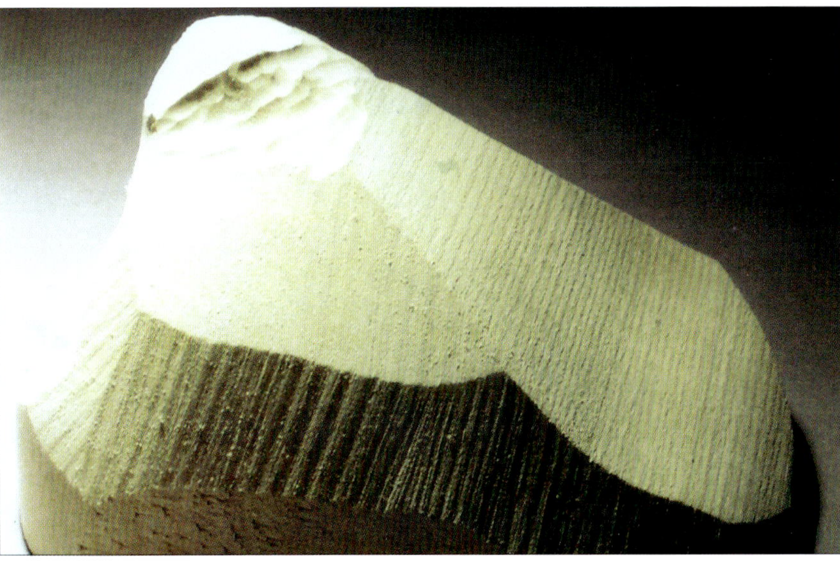

2 I begin by shaping the head with a stump-cutter in my flexible-shaft grinder.

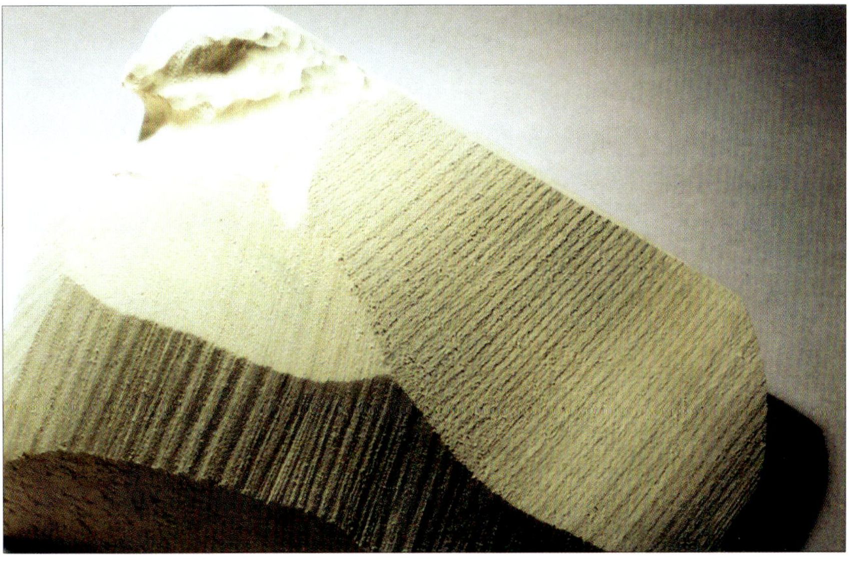

3 In this photo the head is rough-shaped, reflecting the attitude I want to portray.

4 Create the eye cavity with a 4-millimeter diamond bullet cutter.

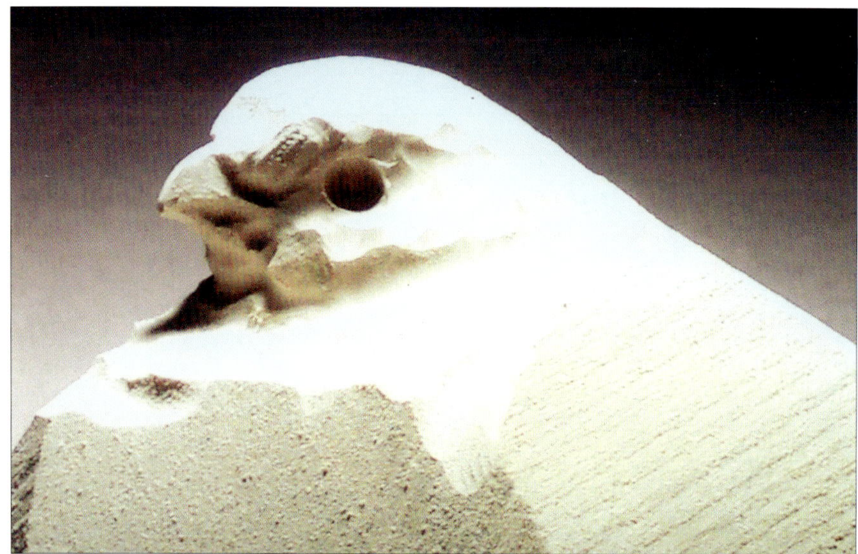

5 At this point the head, bill, and eye cavity have all been rough-shaped with a stump-cutter.

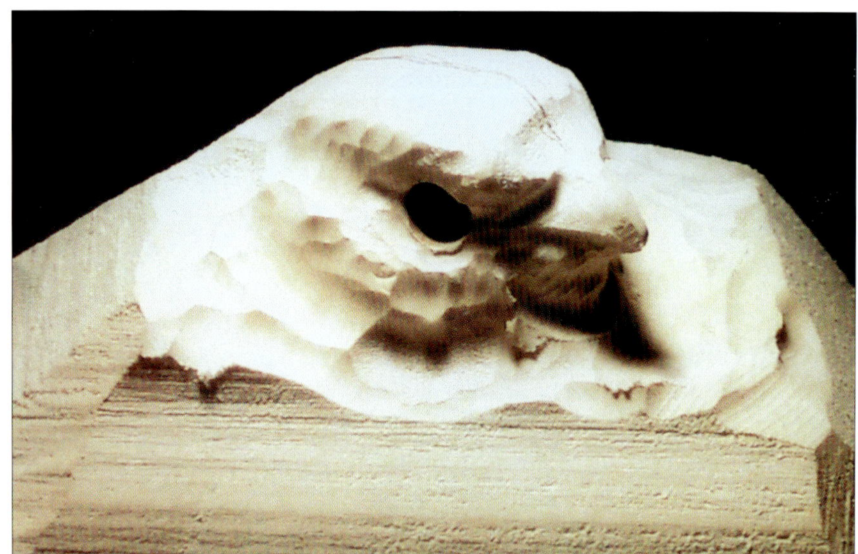

6 Insert the eyes using the same method as was used on the woodcock.

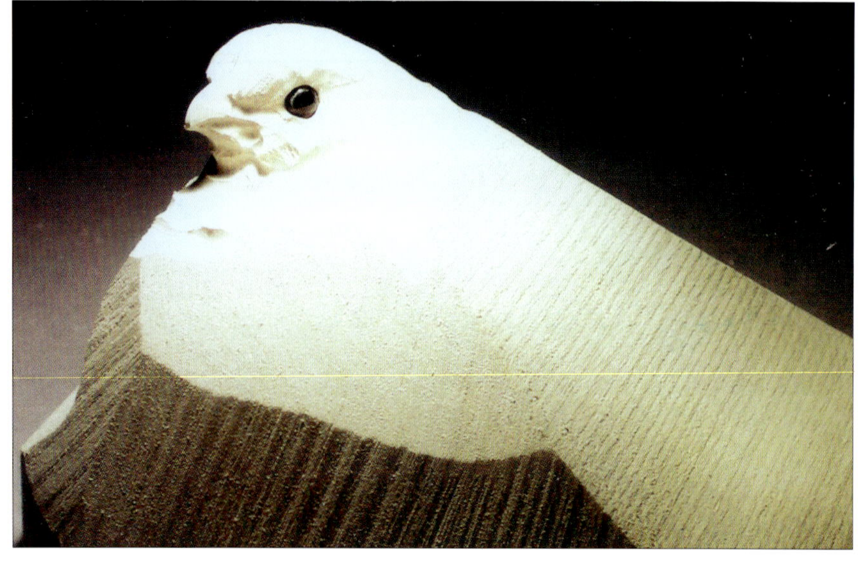

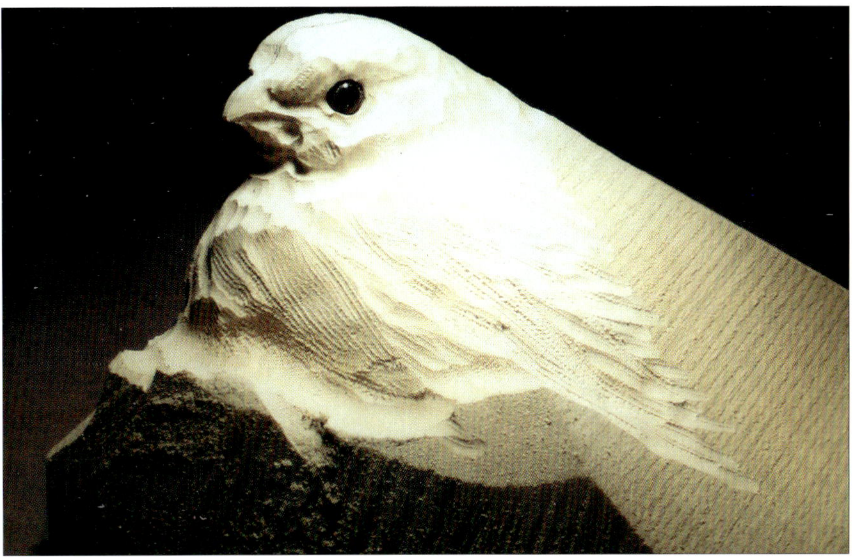

7 I begin to shape the body, starting with the breast.

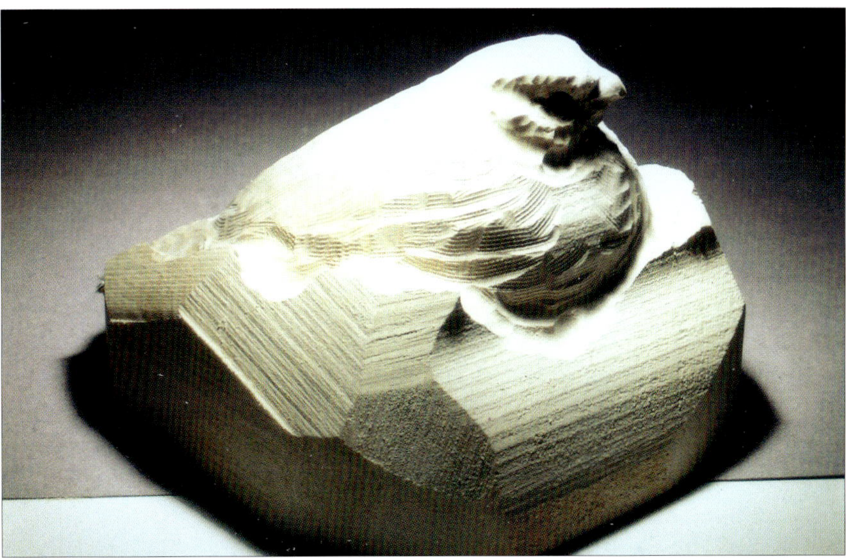

8 The side of the bird has been roughed out. Be careful to pay close attention to your reference material so that you do not remove too much wood too quickly. A 14-millimeter Kutzall or Typhoon burr can be used for the initial removal of wood, but an 8- or 10-millimeter stump-cutter will produce a smoother carving.

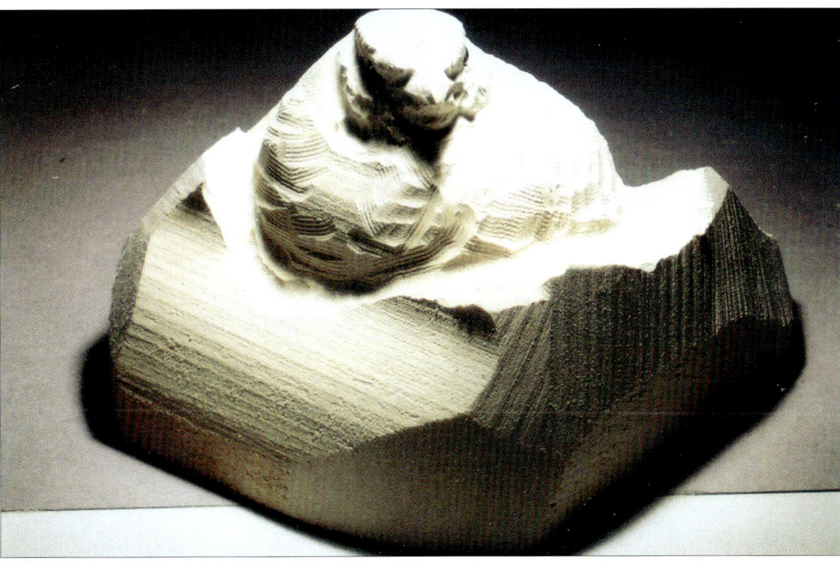

9 Here is a front view of the roughed-out bobwhite.

10 Here is a view from the opposite side.

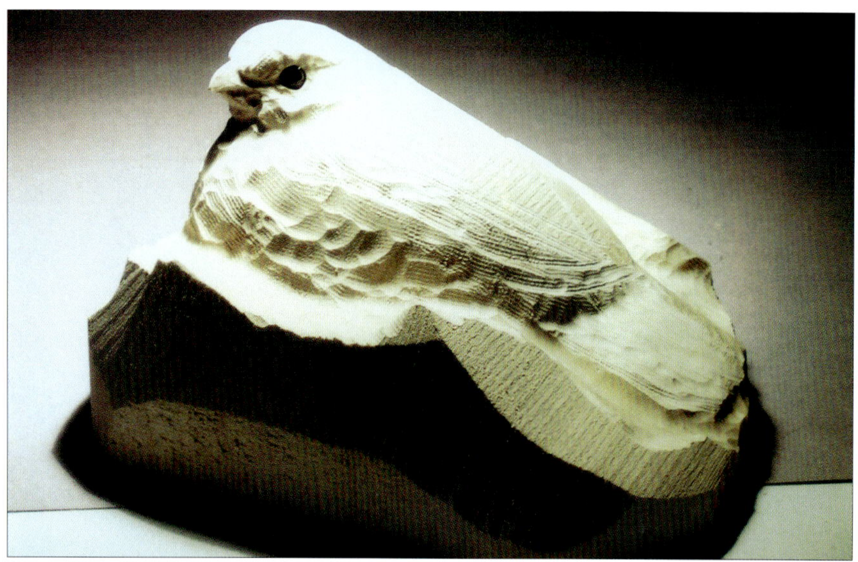

11 In this photo I have roughed out the tail.

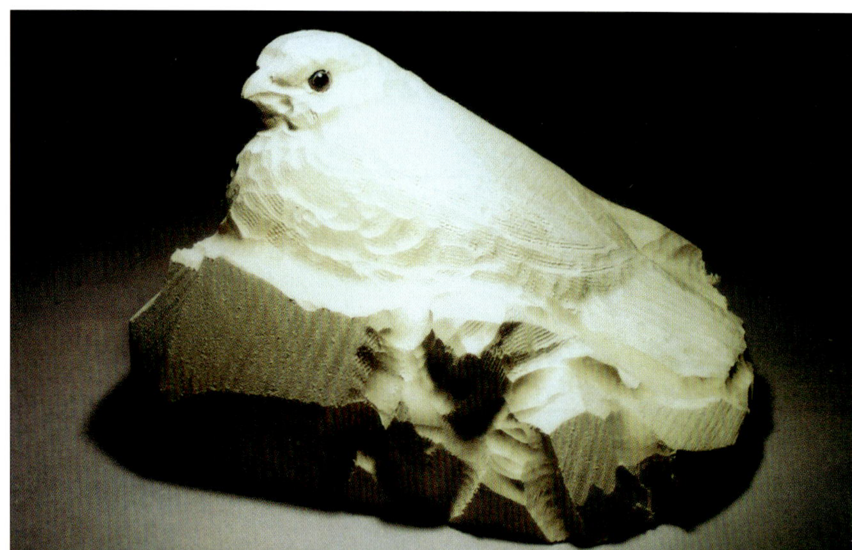

12 With the bird rough-carved, I begin working on the habitat. I used a flat-edged stump-cutter to shape the rocks in the foreground. I then made indentations in the rocks with the round tip of a 4-millimeter diamond bullet cutter.

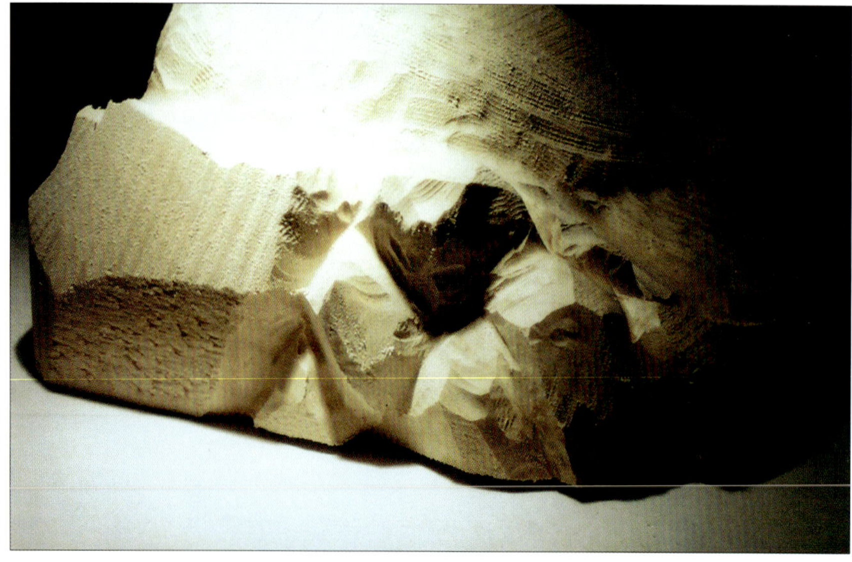

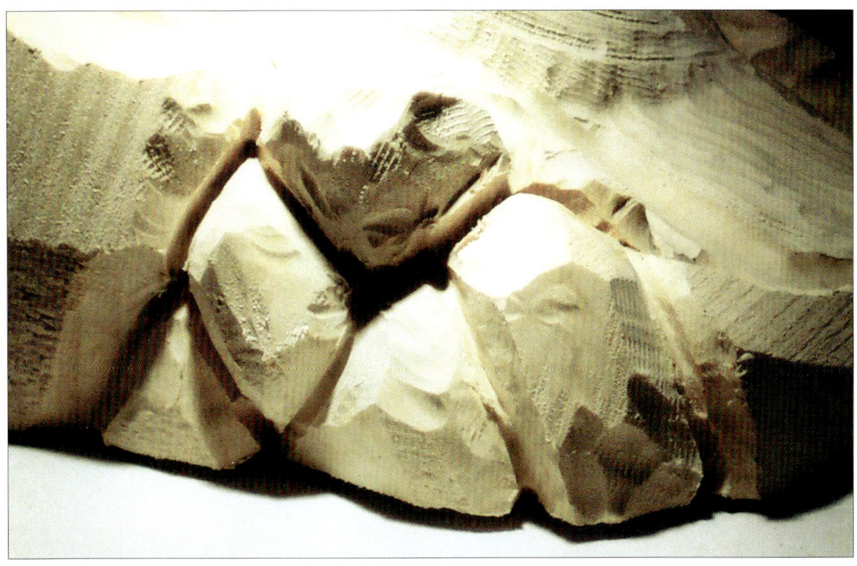

13 Here is a closer view of the rocks taking shape. The key here is to create a pleasing random pattern within the arrangement of rocks.

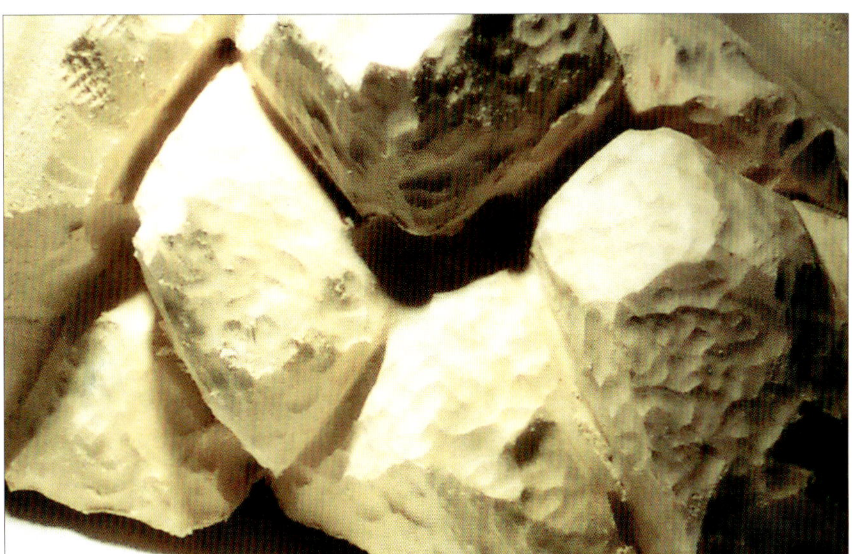

14 After shaping the jumble of rocks I add detail to the individual rocks with the flat-edged stump-cutter (crevices between rocks) and the diamond bullet (indentations in rocks). Later I will paint the rocks with a wash of a mix of Jo Sonja's Burnt Umber and Liquitex Ultramarine Blue. Once again, the carver determines the amount of each color used to adjust it to his or her liking. You have to experiment—test it out on paper first.

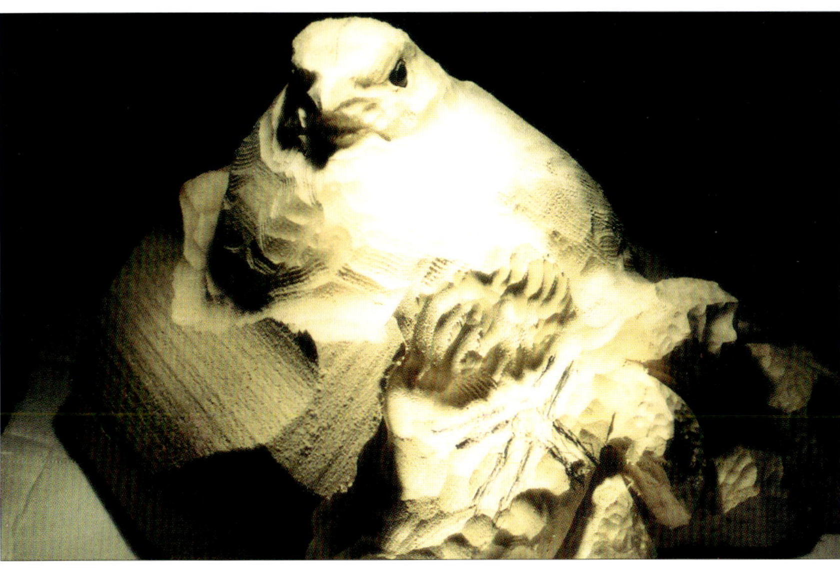

15 Before carving out the bobwhite's feet I mark their eventual position so I can envision their placement within the composition. I usually save the carving of the feet until after I have completed the carving of most of the bird.

16 I use a stump-cutter to rough-shape the feet according to my measurements and other reference material.

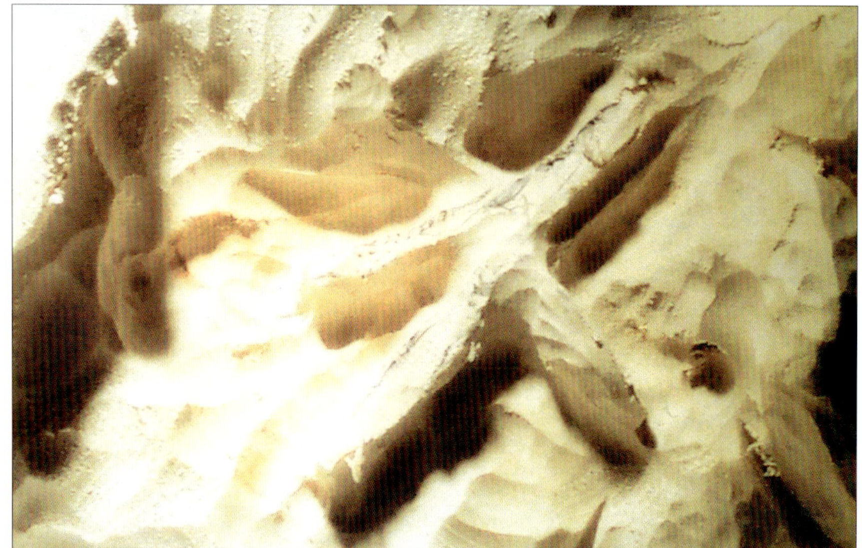

17 The feet are ready for sanding in preparation for the addition of texture.

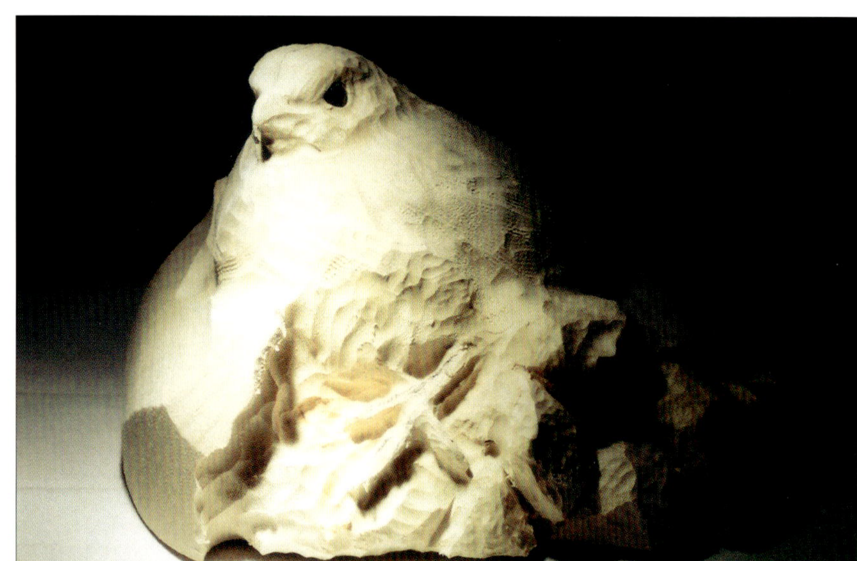

18 Here is a top view of the bobwhite's left foot with the details added. The most important of these are the scales on the tops of the feet and the reticulations on their pads. I use a special "reticulation bit" in my micromotor to carve the latter of these areas, making a multitude of small, round impressions on the lower halves of the toes. The scales are carved by making horizontal cuts in the tops of the toes with a combination of diamond bullet and diamond needle bits.

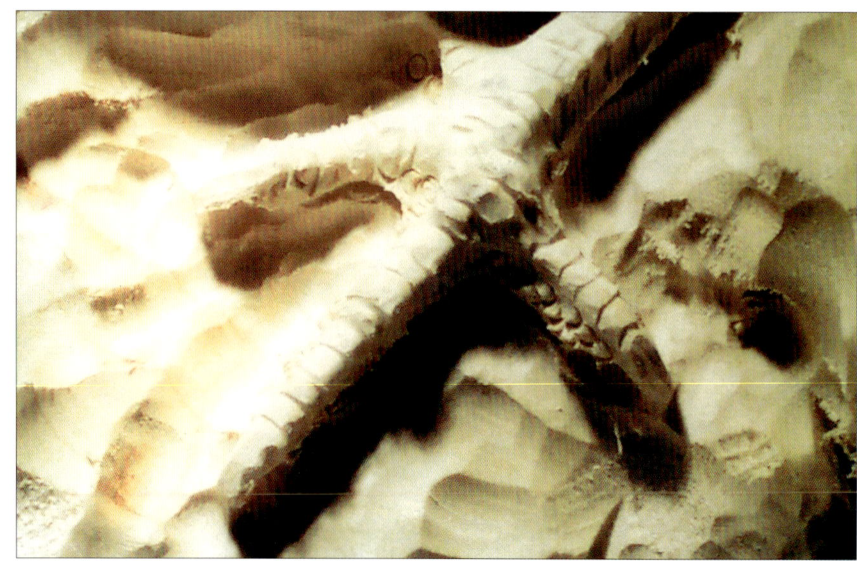

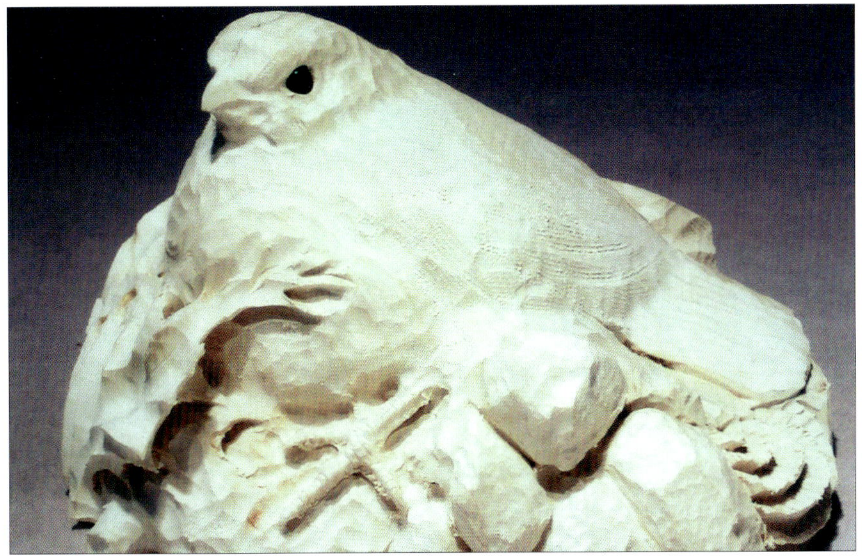

19 This photo shows the foot completed. If you happen to damage one of the toes it can be repaired with a solution of baking soda and instant cyanoacrylate (CA) glue sprayed on with accelerator. Then you can sand the toe smooth and paint it with a wash of matte medium and Warm Black pigment.

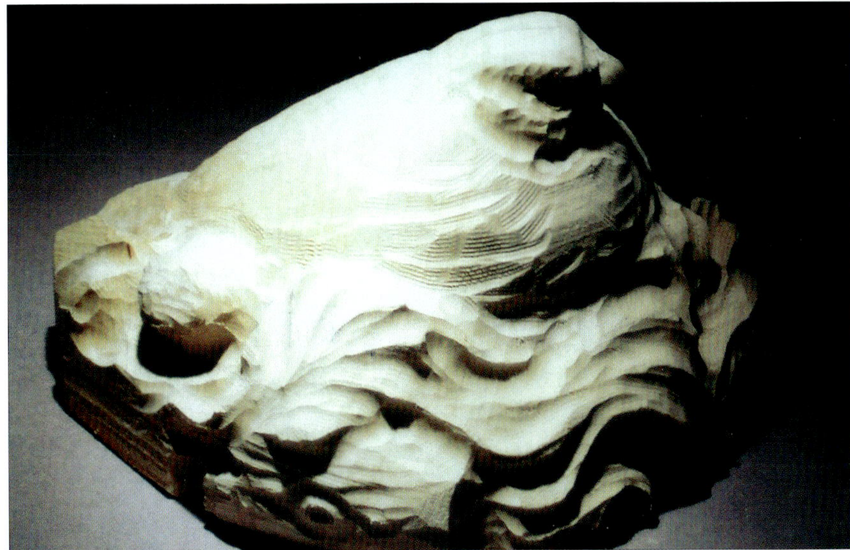

20 On my bobwhite's right side I decided to add a few leaves, establishing their general shape as seen in this photo.

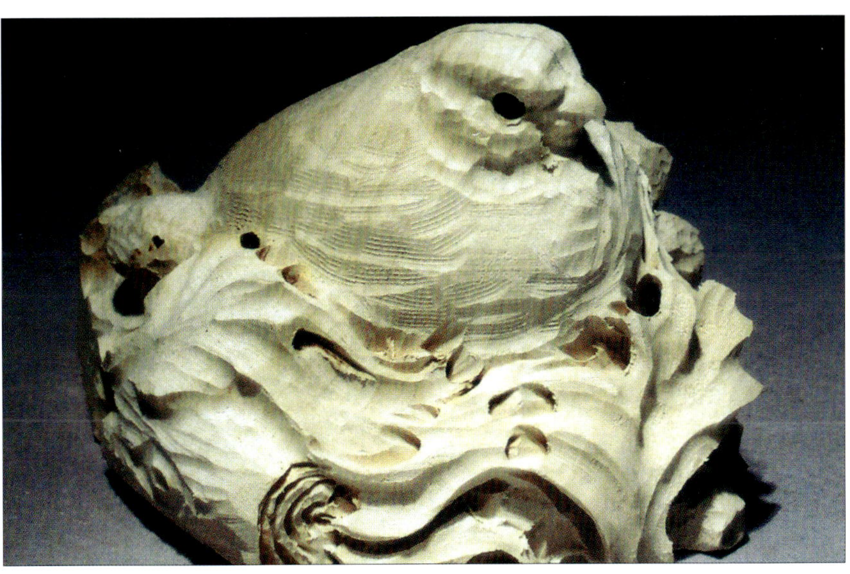

21 In this photo the leaves are beginning to take on a more finite shape. The various features of any given habitat within a bird carving are determined by two main factors: the creative imagination of the carver, and his or her research of the habitat of the subject species. Within these parameters the possibilities are endless. In many cases the shape of the wood itself will dictate which habitat features to include. Then it's just a matter of sketching them in and removing the excess wood.

22 I added lichens to the arrangement, layering and fluting them with a 3-millimeter diamond bullet.

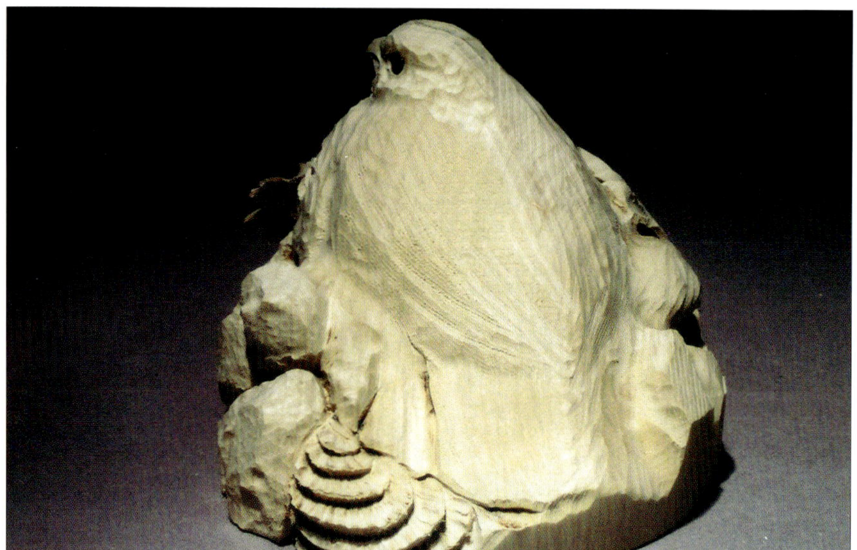

23 Here is a front view of the carved composition. Seal the bird with a 50/50 solution of lacquer and lacquer thinner. Apply this solution moderately; you don't want the surface of the carving to be too shiny.

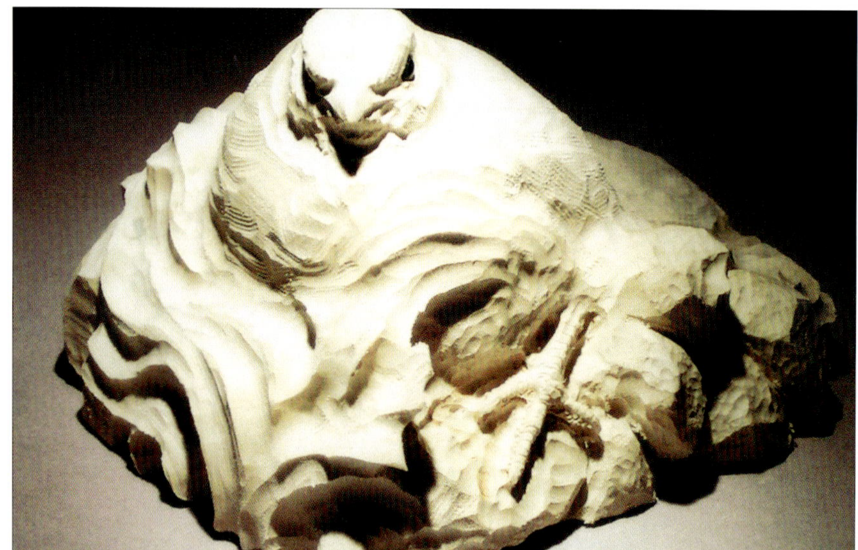

BURNING AND PAINTING THE BOBWHITE QUAIL

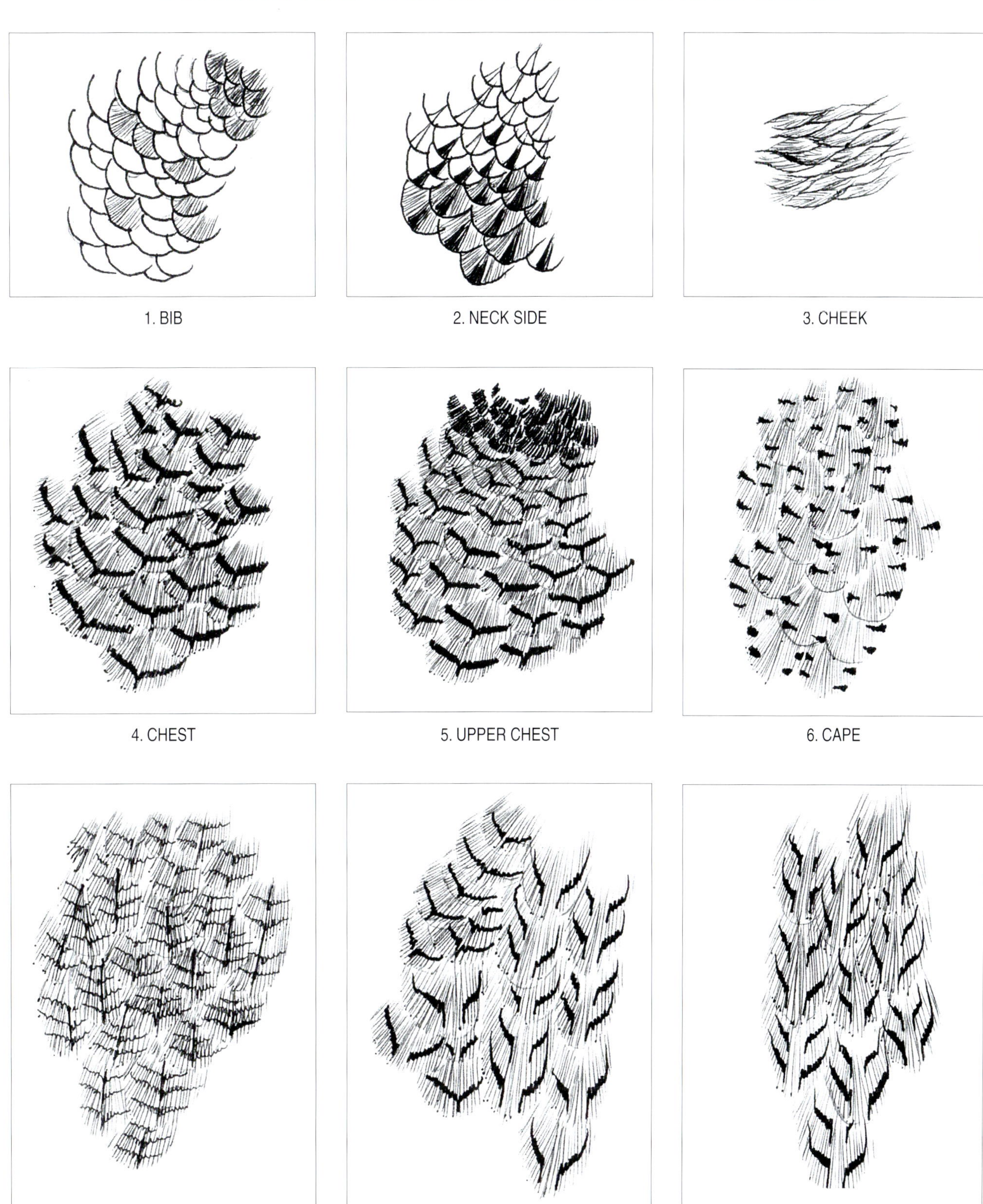

Figure 1 Here are the various types of feathers you will try to recreate on your quail carving through the painting and burning processes. Especially for beginners it is wise to practice burning and painting the groups individually on scrap wood before attempting them on the actual carving.

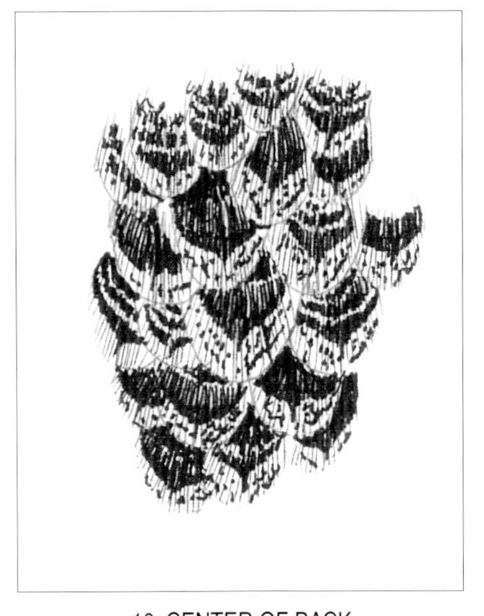

10. CENTER OF BACK

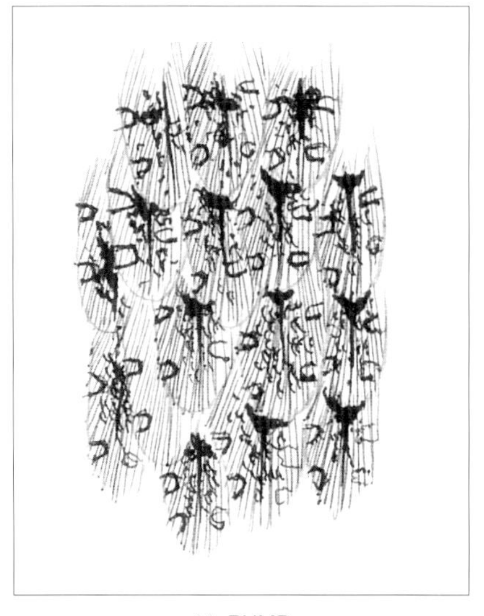

11. RUMP

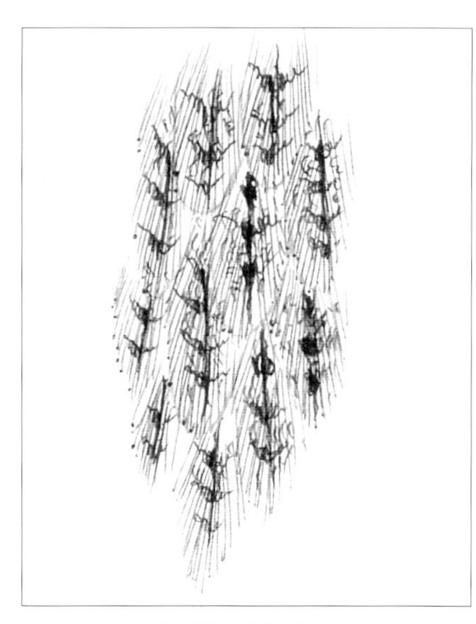

12. TAIL COVERTS

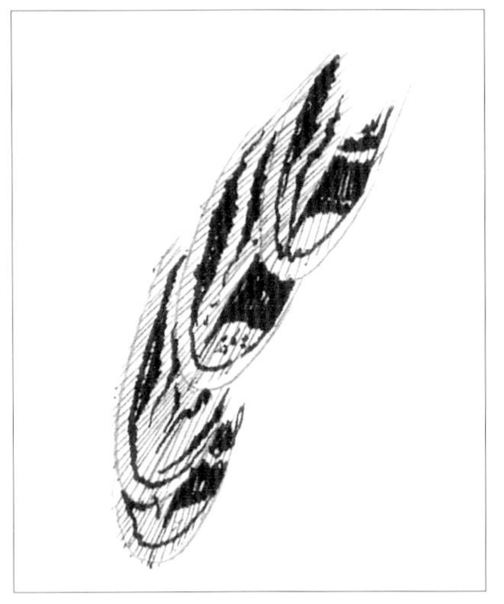

13. SCAPULARS

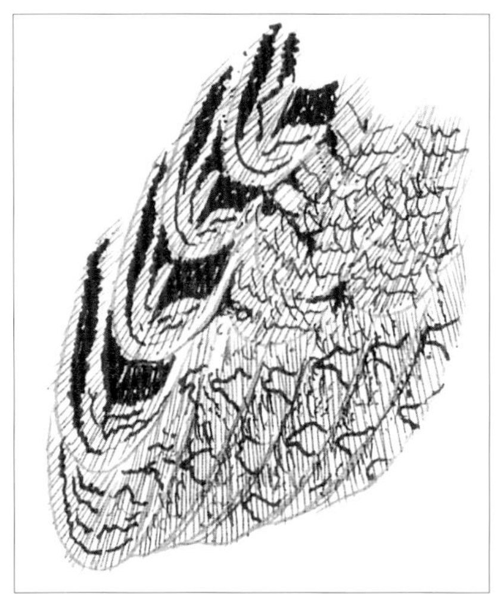

14. SECONDARIES

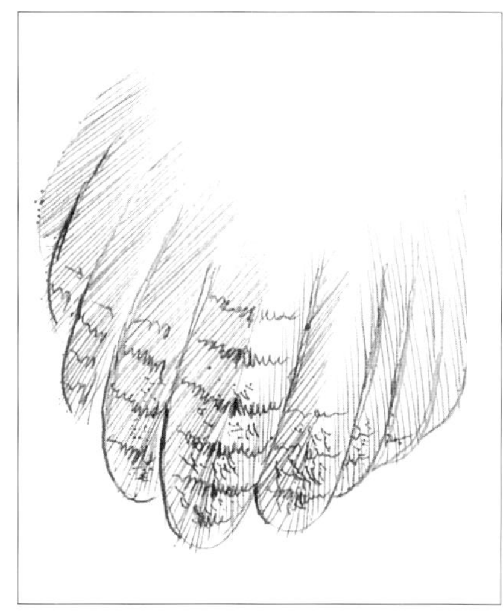

15. TAIL

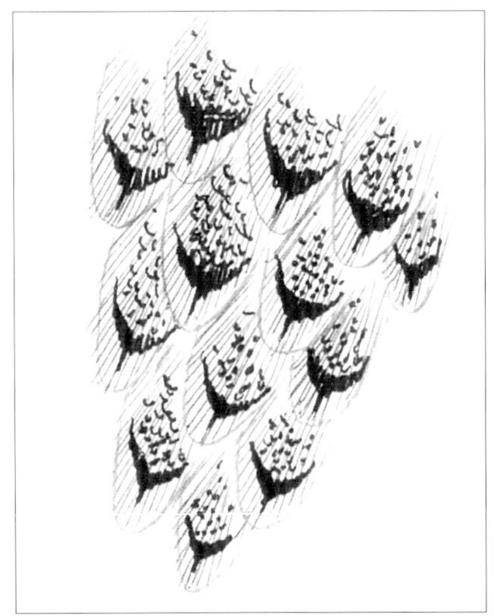

16. UNDER TAIL

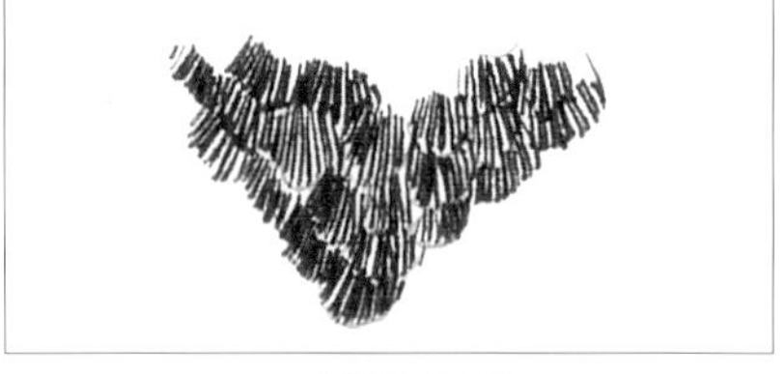

17. UNDER BIB

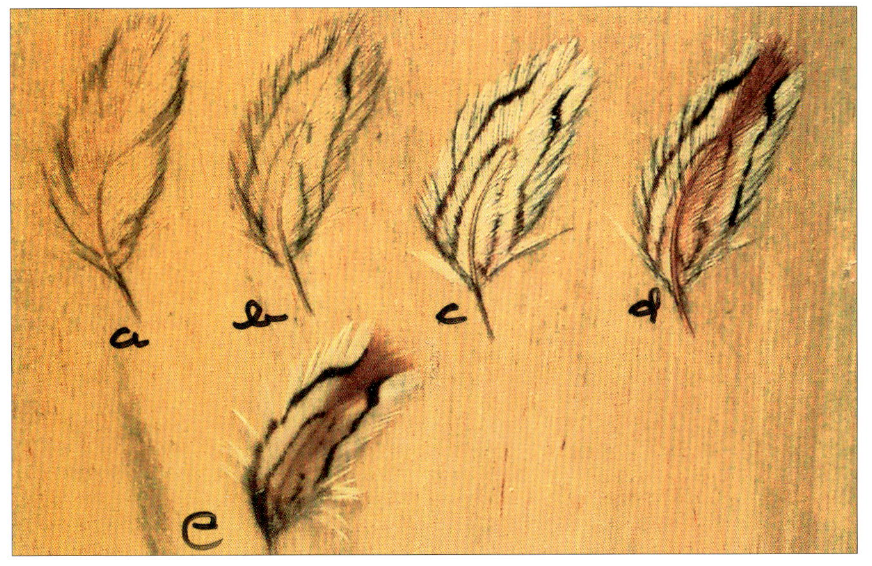

1 This photo shows the process I use for woodburning and painting a bobwhite quail feather.

a. First, pencil in the feather outline.

b. Burn the dark areas of the feather according to your sketch.

c. Paint gesso mixed 50/50 with water in-between the burn lines.

d. Paint the center of the feather with the appropriate color (in this case Burnt Sienna).

e. Here is a real quail feather, the appearance you are striving for.

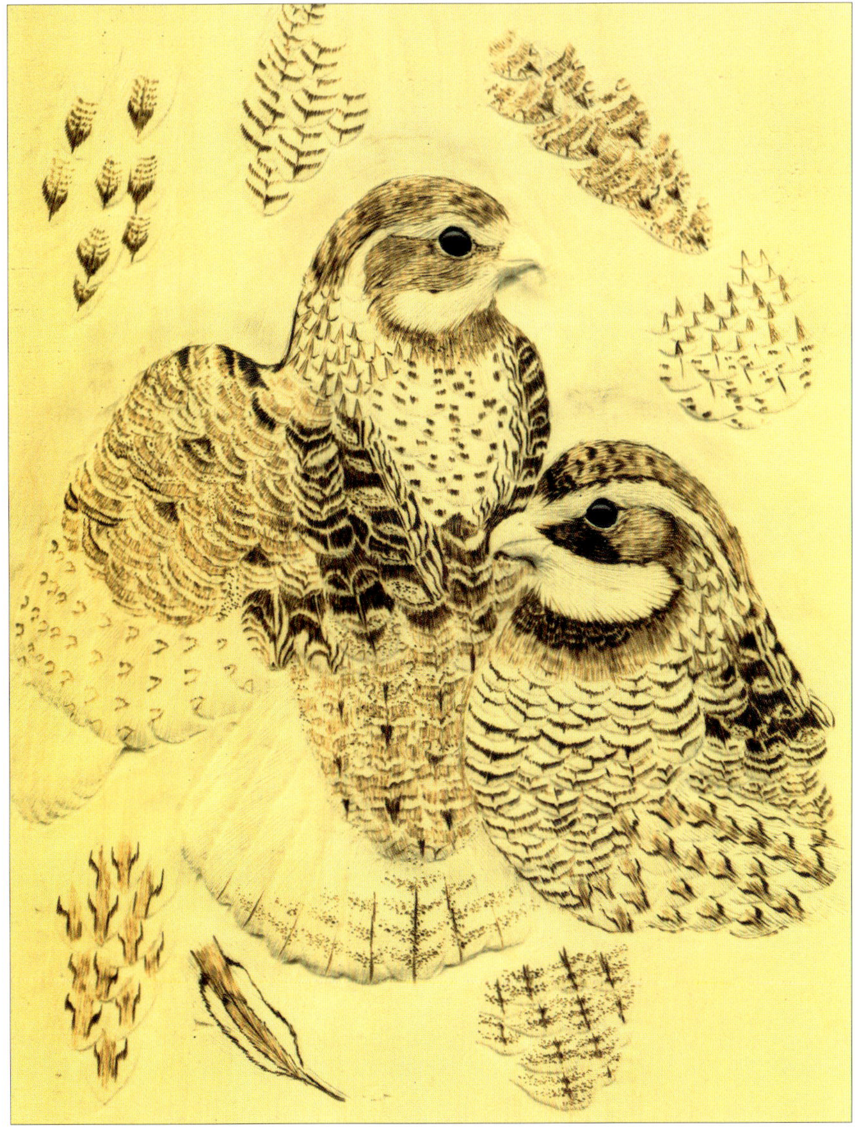

2 Burn in detail on the bobwhite according to the patterns shown here using tight, fine strokes. The left bird is a female of the species and the right one is a male. The two have slightly different feather markings.

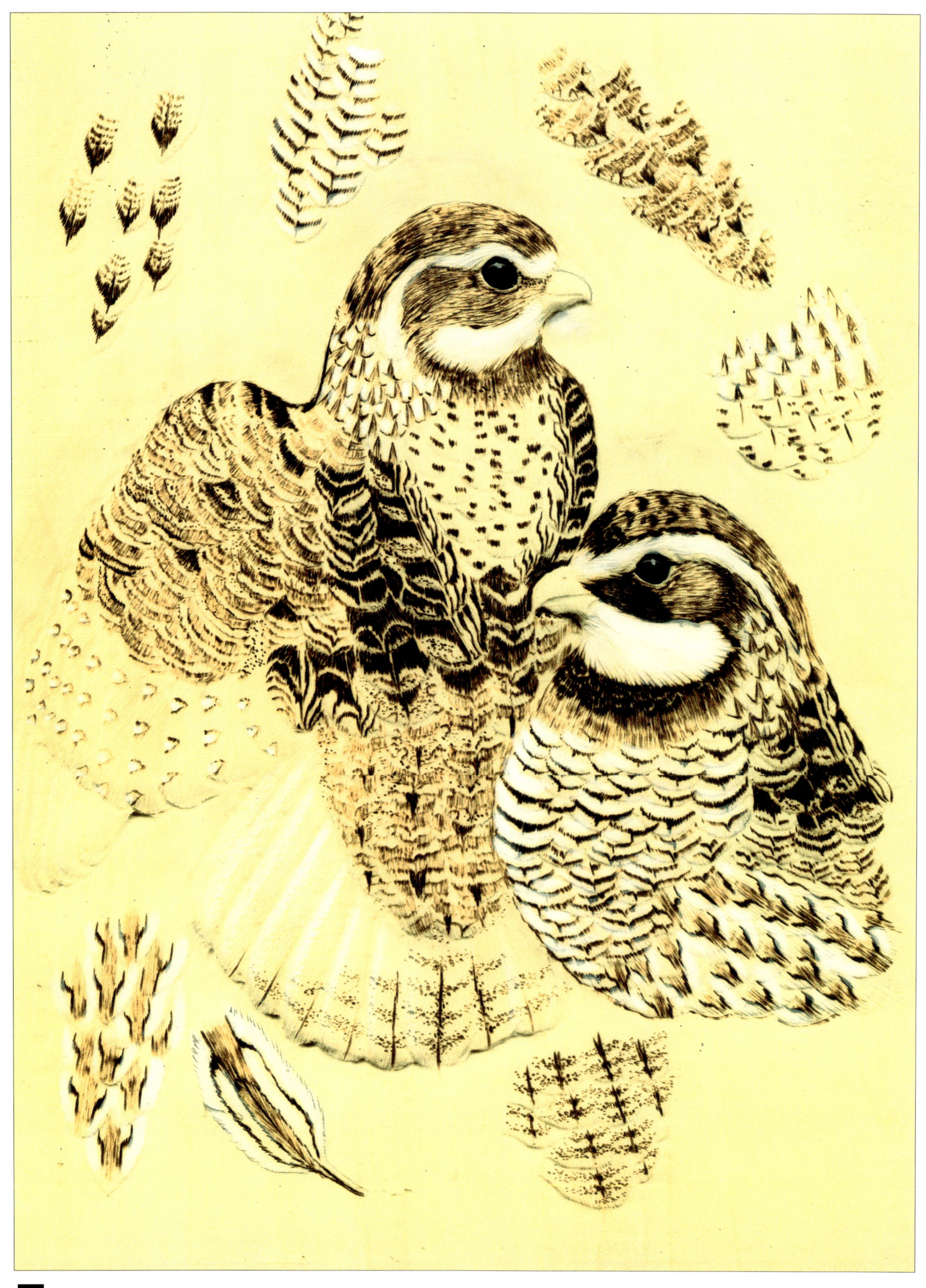

3 Then paint in the white areas of the quail with gesso as shown here.

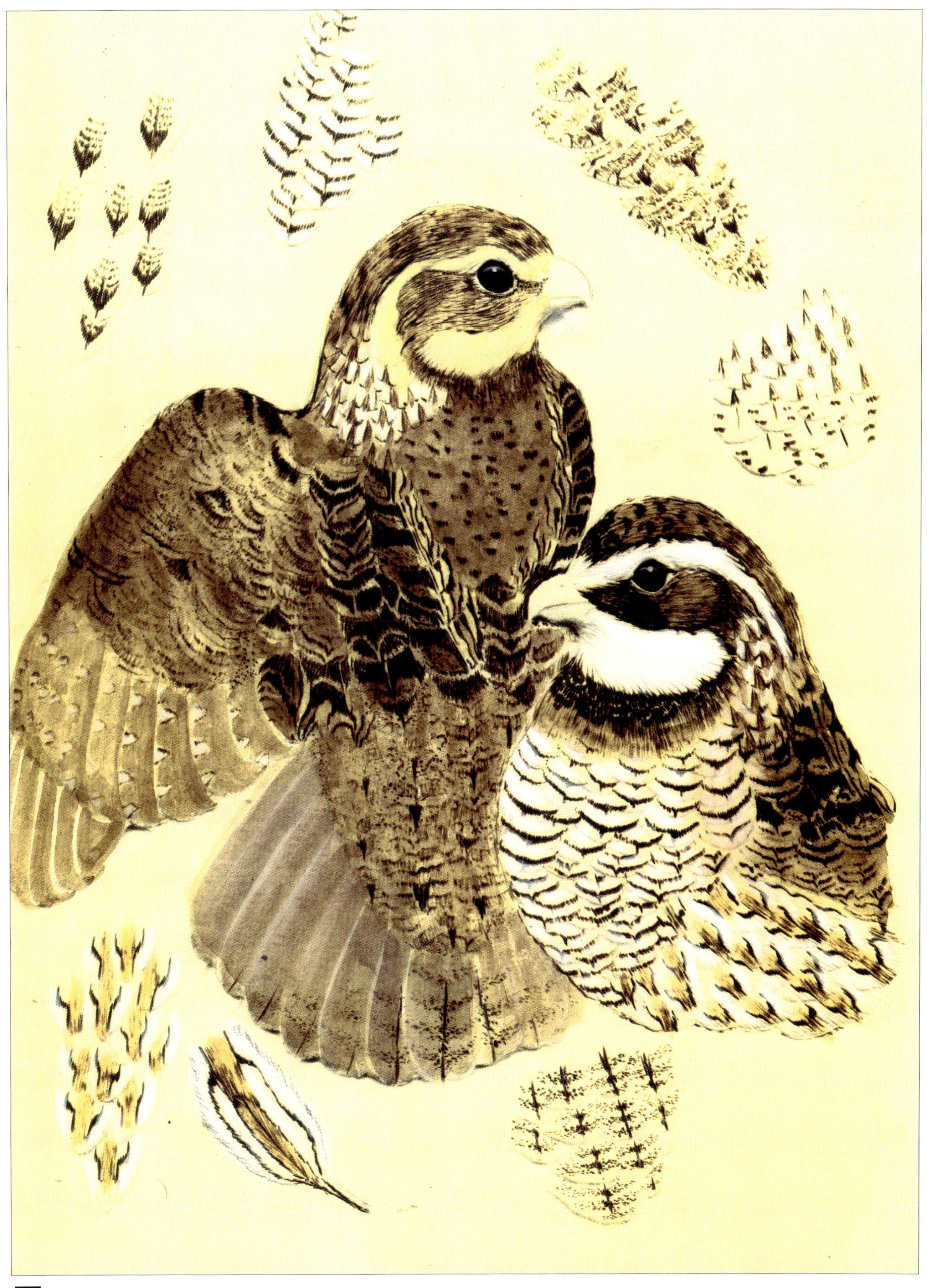

4 This version shows the completed painting of the quail's plumage, which you can use as a guide as you go through the following steps.

5 Paint the chin and bib area with a mix of Titanium White and a touch of Raw Umber, then paint the feathers below the white bib with Warm Black. The circle under the bib area must be painted with washes of Burnt Umber, and the breast feathers can be completed with Titanium White and an edging of Warm Black. I use either a #2 or #3 brush in this area.

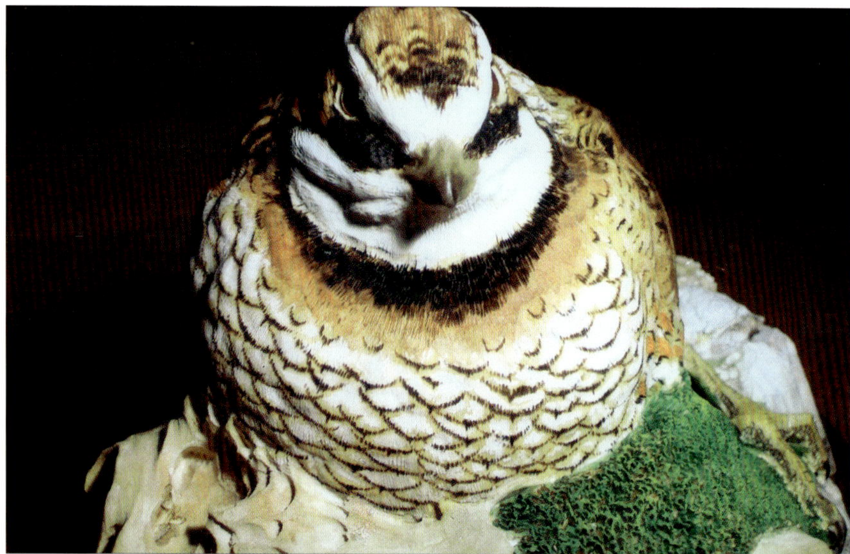

6 This side view shows a close-up of the eye and bib area.

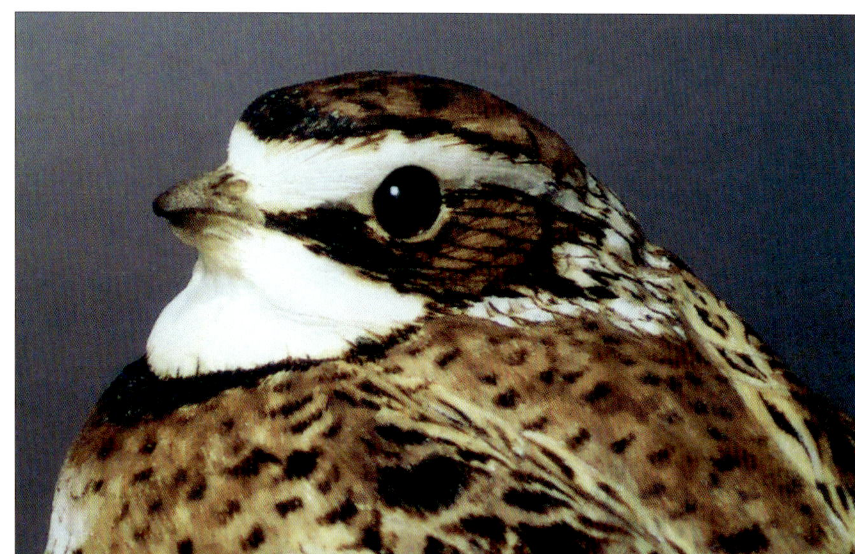

7 The feathers of the sides and lower back of the neck are painted Titanium White with a Burnt Umber *V* in the center of each feather. Paint the side pocket feathers Titanium White and then paint a mixture of Burnt Sienna and Burnt Umber in the center of each feather. Paint the markings on the edges of the feathers Warm Black.

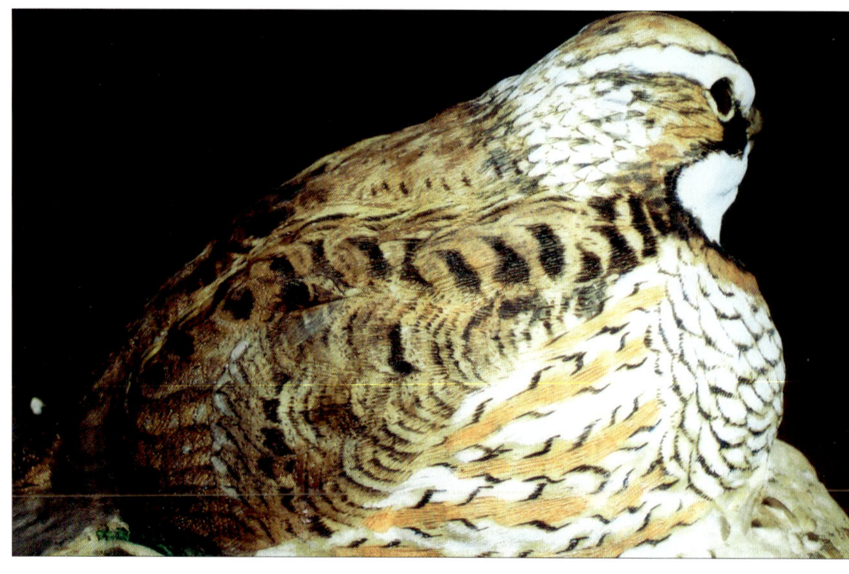

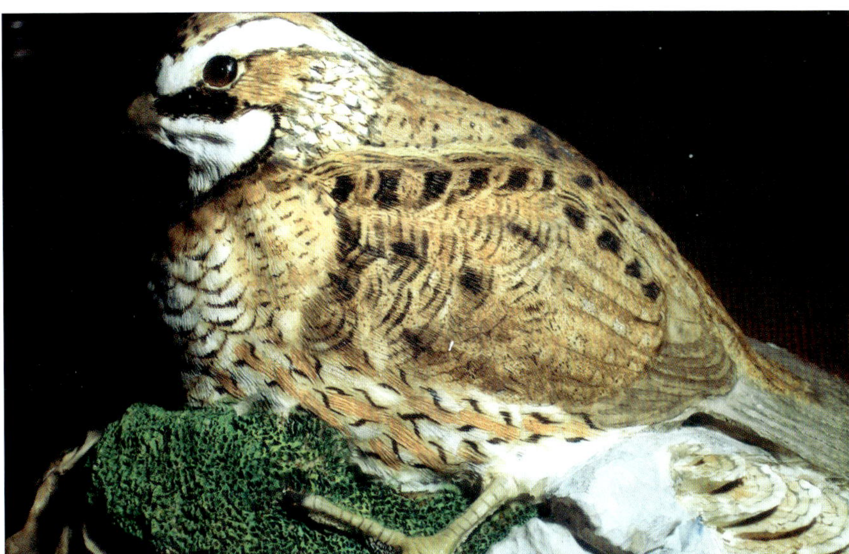

8 Paint the cheeks with a wash of Raw Umber. Then paint the front of the cheeks and around the bib area with Warm Black.

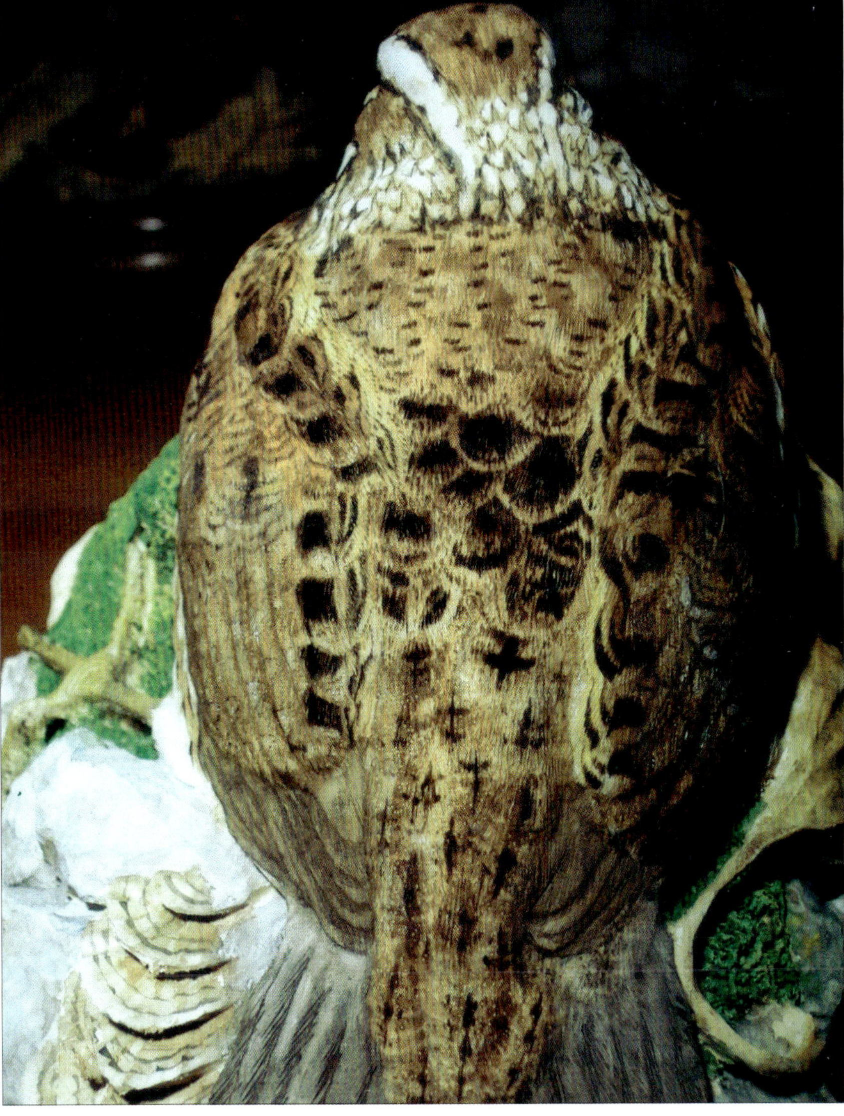

9 Paint the cape with a wash of Raw Umber and just a touch of Ultramarine Blue.

10 Paint the wing coverts with a wash of Burnt Umber and a touch of Ultramarine Blue. The chest feathers next to the side pockets are Titanium White with the mixture of Burnt Sienna and Burnt Umber in their centers. Paint black markings on the edges of these feathers.

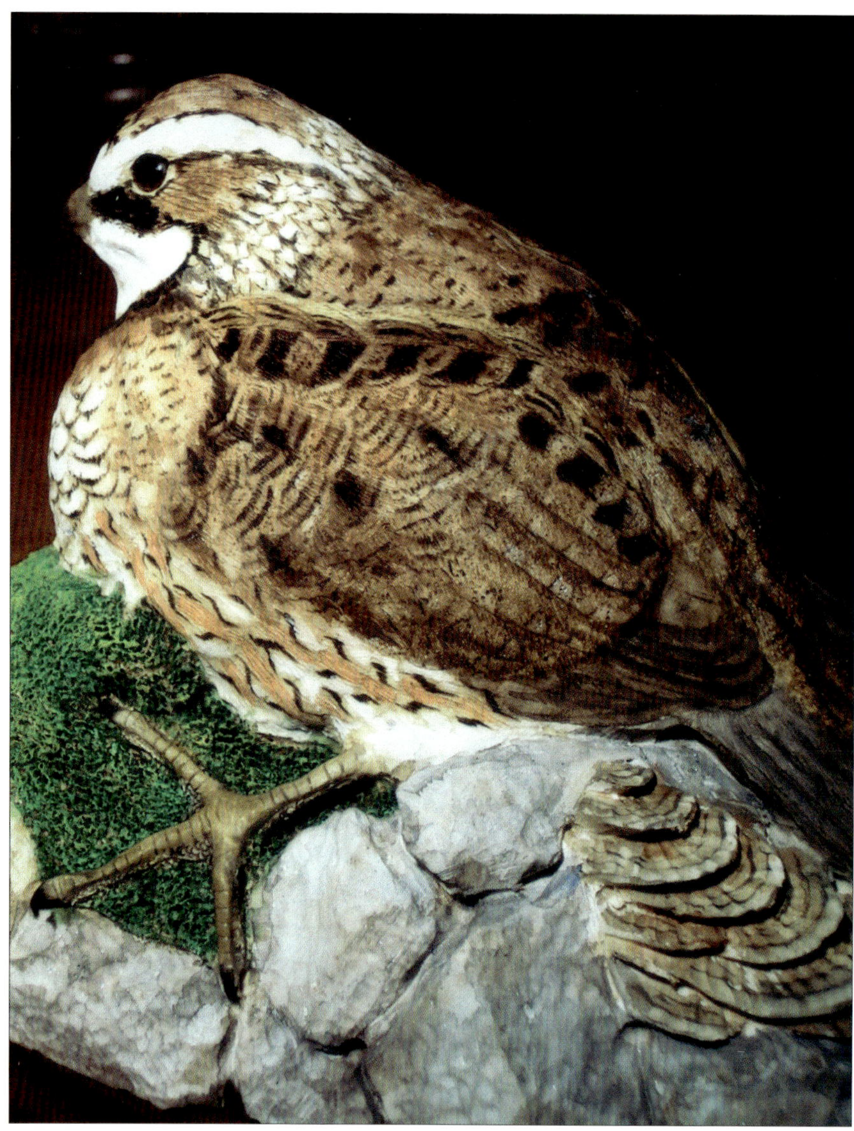

11 In the center of the bobwhite's back below the cape, paint the center of each feather with Burnt Umber and the outside edges of the feathers with Titanium White. Paint the darkly burned markings with Warm Black.

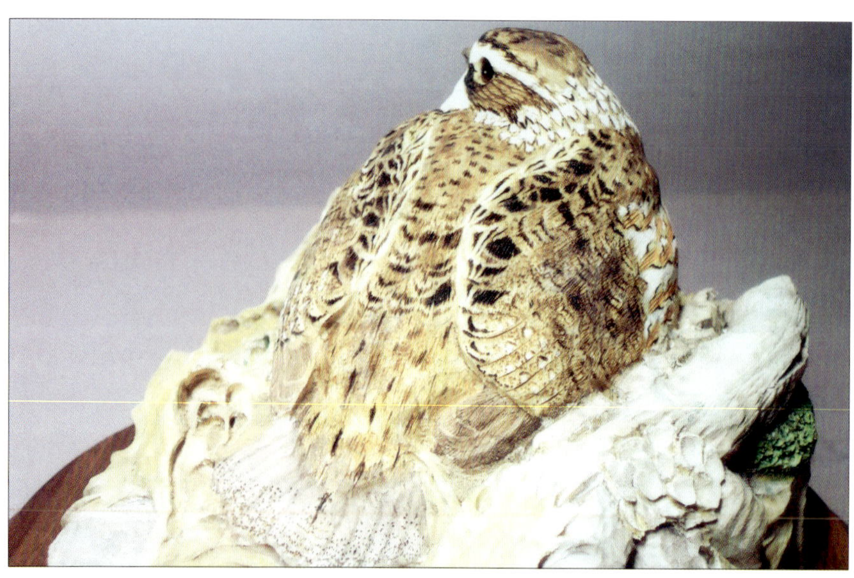

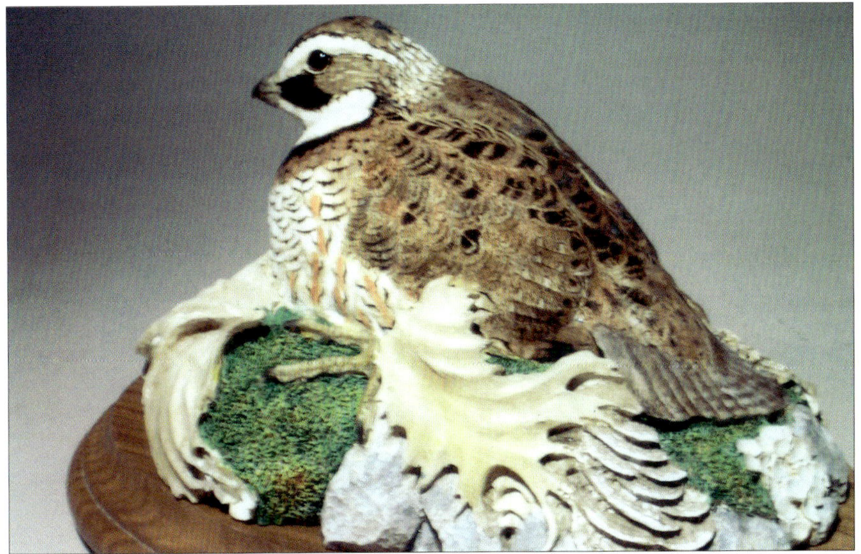

12 On the rump, paint in the Warm Black markings, then wash the entire area with the Burnt Umber/Ultramarine Blue mix. Use this same wash to paint the rocks in the habitat, and wipe certain areas (especially the edges) with a damp rag to create a light shade of the color. Wash mossy areas with Moss Green, and then with Cadmium Yellow Medium. The rippled parts of the lichens are painted with a wash of a mixture of Jo Sonja's Warm White and a touch of Raw Umber. Then the edges are painted with Raw Umber in a consistency slightly thicker than a wash.

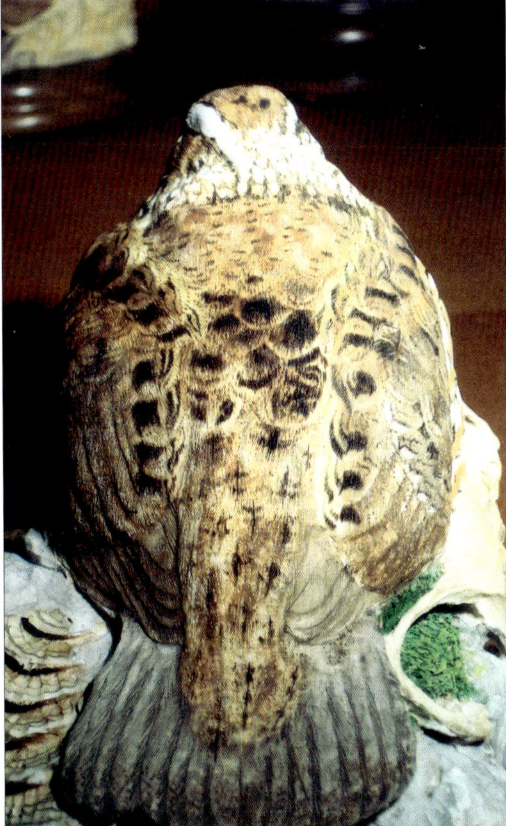

13 Use the same system as described in the last step to paint the tail and tail coverts. Paint the markings Warm Black and then apply a wash of Burnt Umber and Ultramarine Blue. On the scapulars, again paint in the Warm Black markings, then paint the centers of the feathers with Burnt Umber and the feather edges with a mixture of Titanium White and just a touch of Raw Umber.

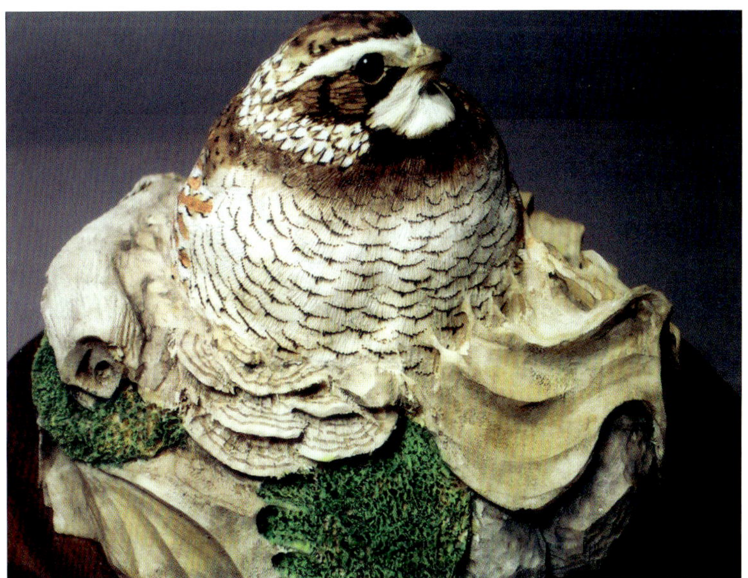

14 Here is a front view of the completed bobwhite quail.

THE EASTERN RUFFED GROUSE

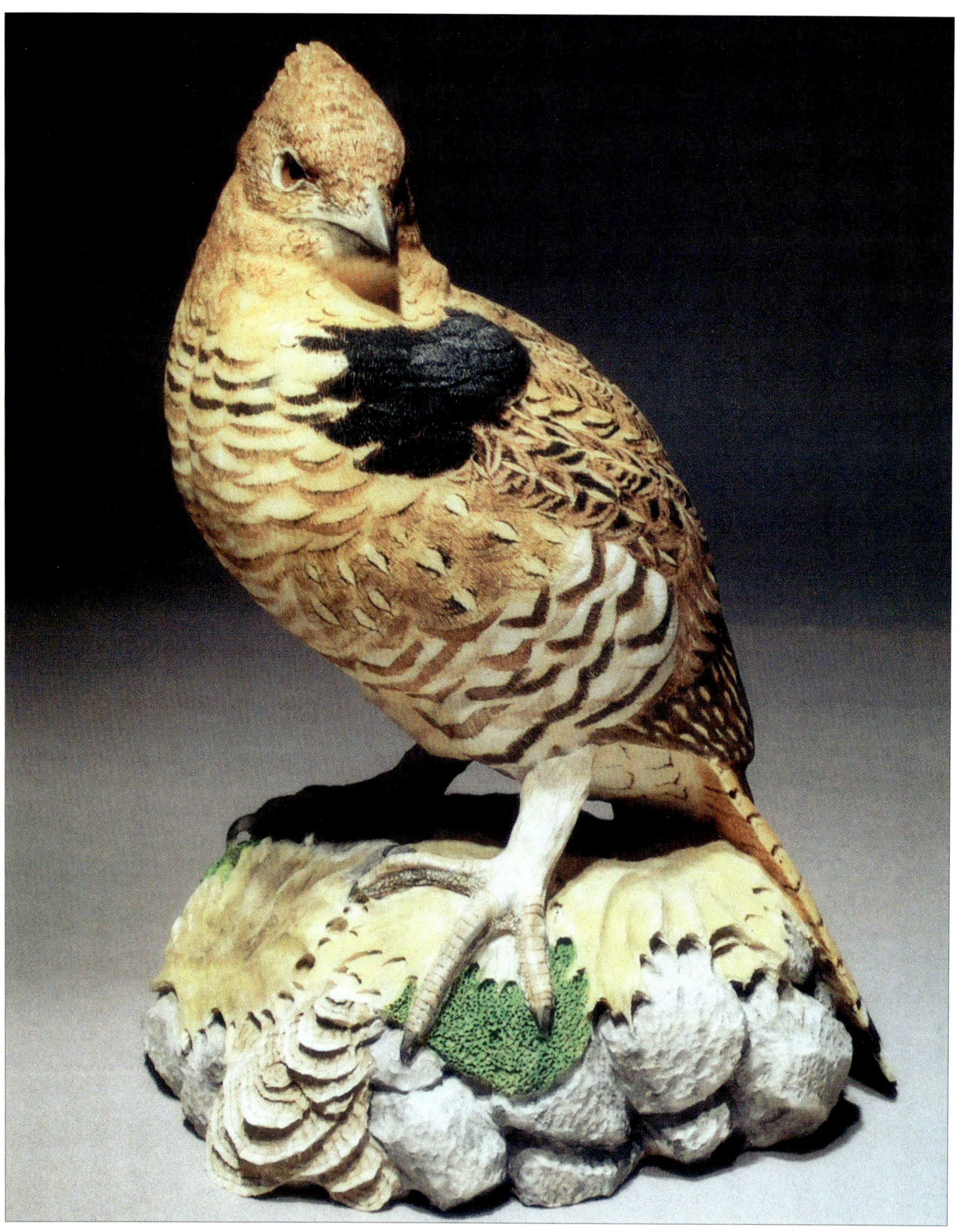

The eastern ruffed grouse is a large red-brown or gray-brown bird that measures 15 to 20 inches in length. The species has become very cautious due to over-hunting, and they tend to roost high in the trees during the summer and autumn months and frequent the ground only in the winter. Ruffed grouse are very hardy birds that can withstand extreme cold and privation. Their diet normally consists of insects, fruits, and nuts, but they have been known to eat the bark off of twigs when desperate for food. You will need a 6- x 8- x 12-inch block of tupelo or other carving wood from which to carve this bird, plus 9-millimeter brown glass eyes to give it life.

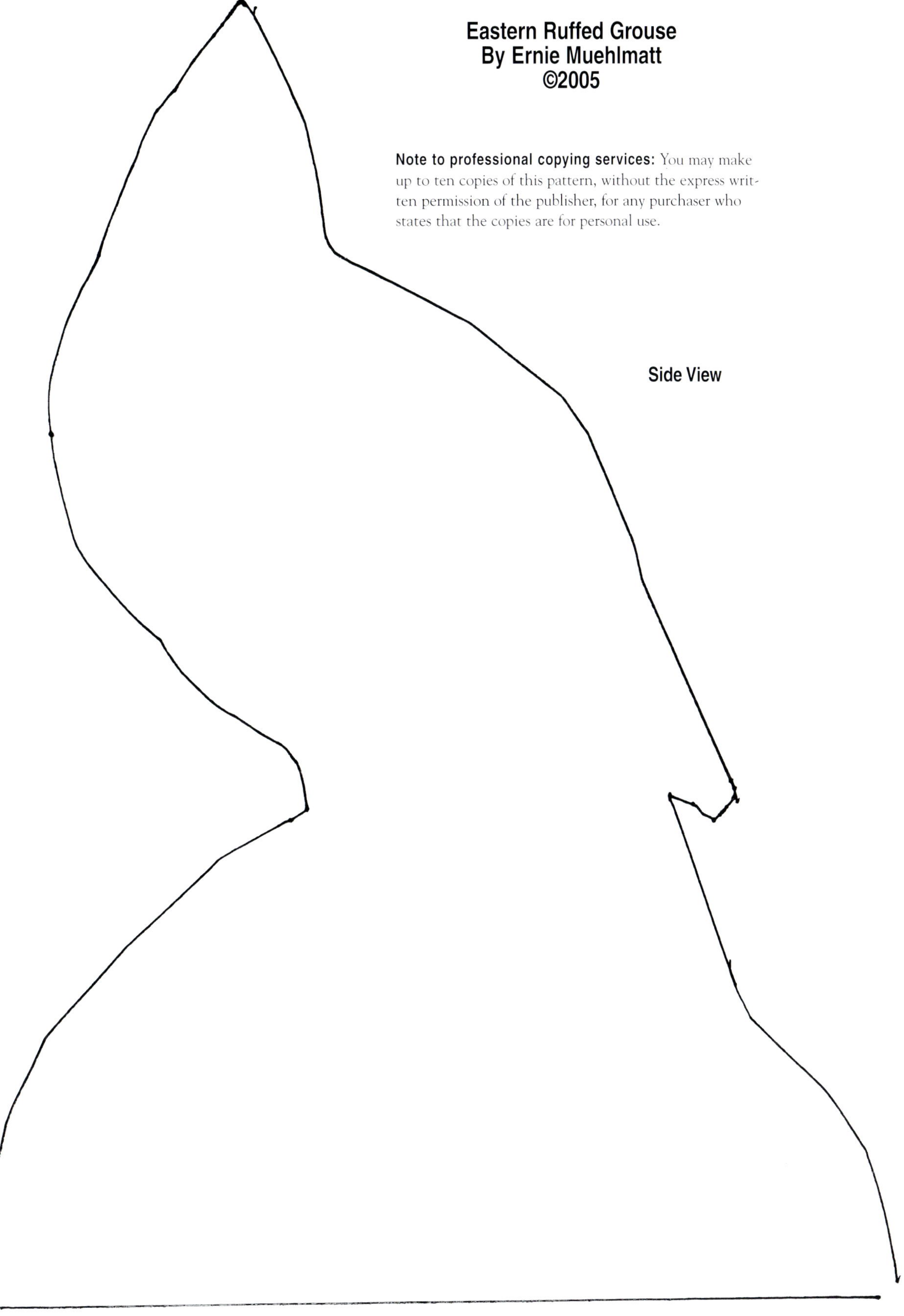
Eastern Ruffed Grouse
By Ernie Muehlmatt
©2005
Note to professional copying services: You may make up to ten copies of this pattern, without the express written permission of the publisher, for any purchaser who states that the copies are for personal use.
Side View

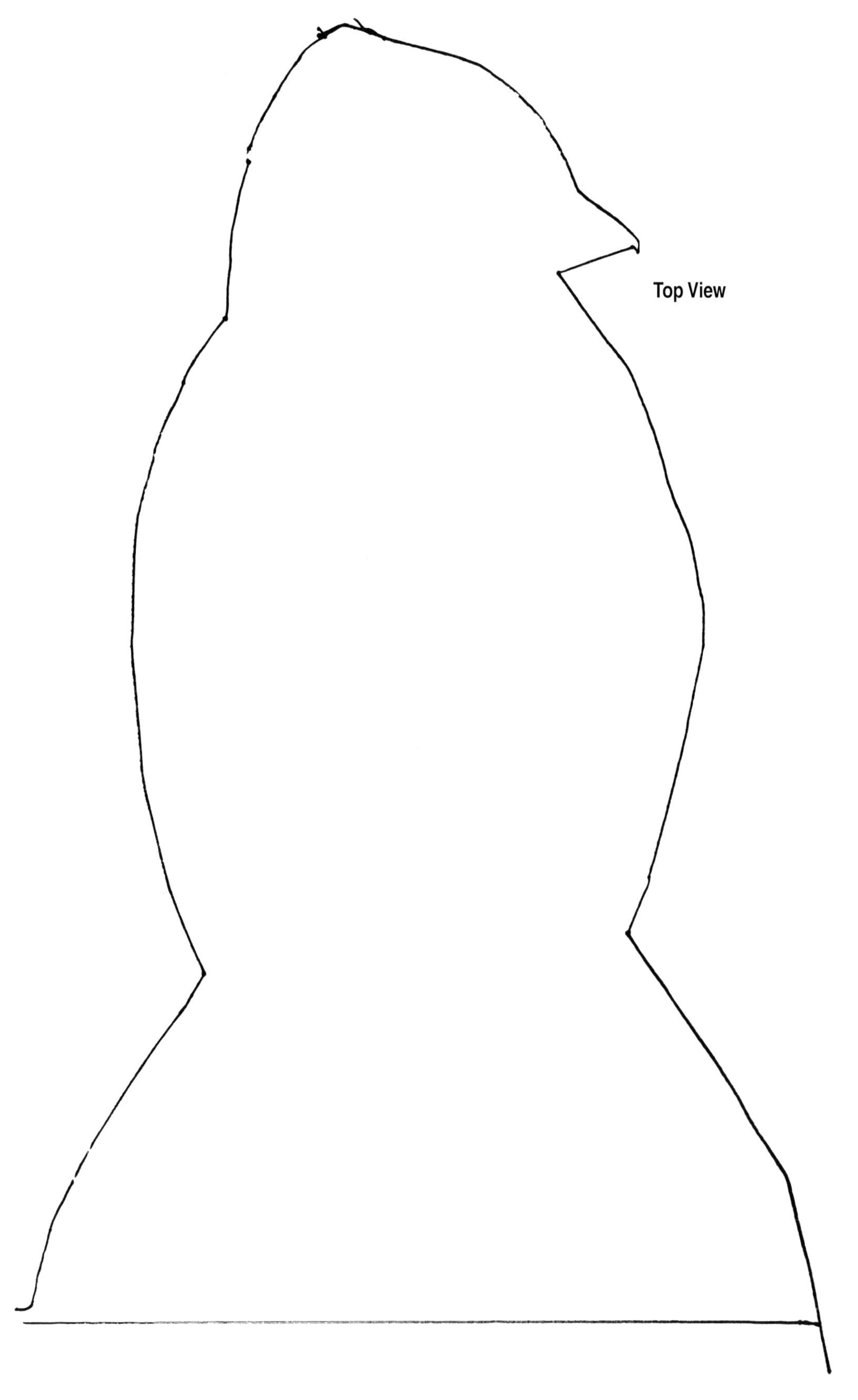
Top View

Head Reference

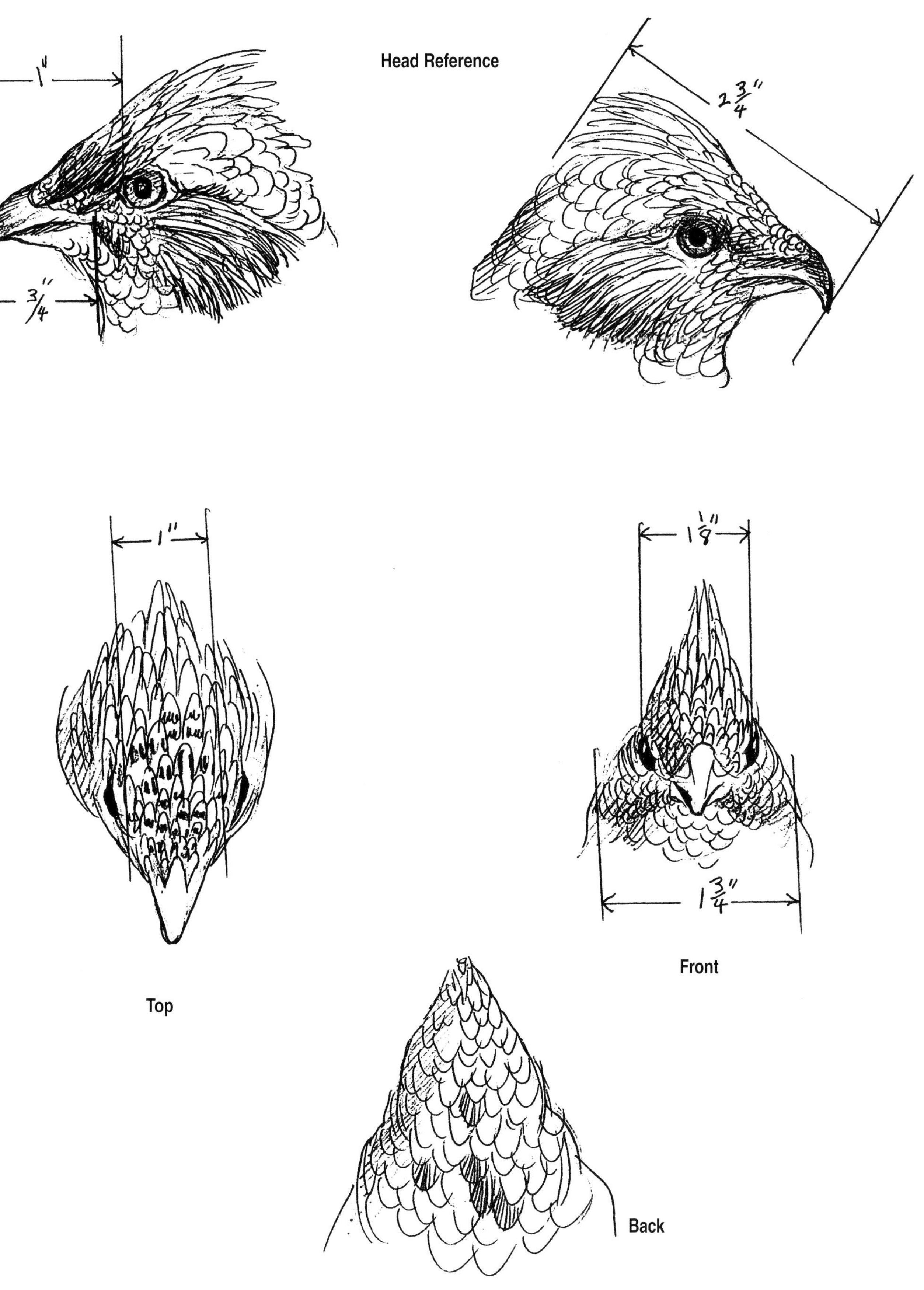

Top

Front

Back

Top of Tail
Feather Layout

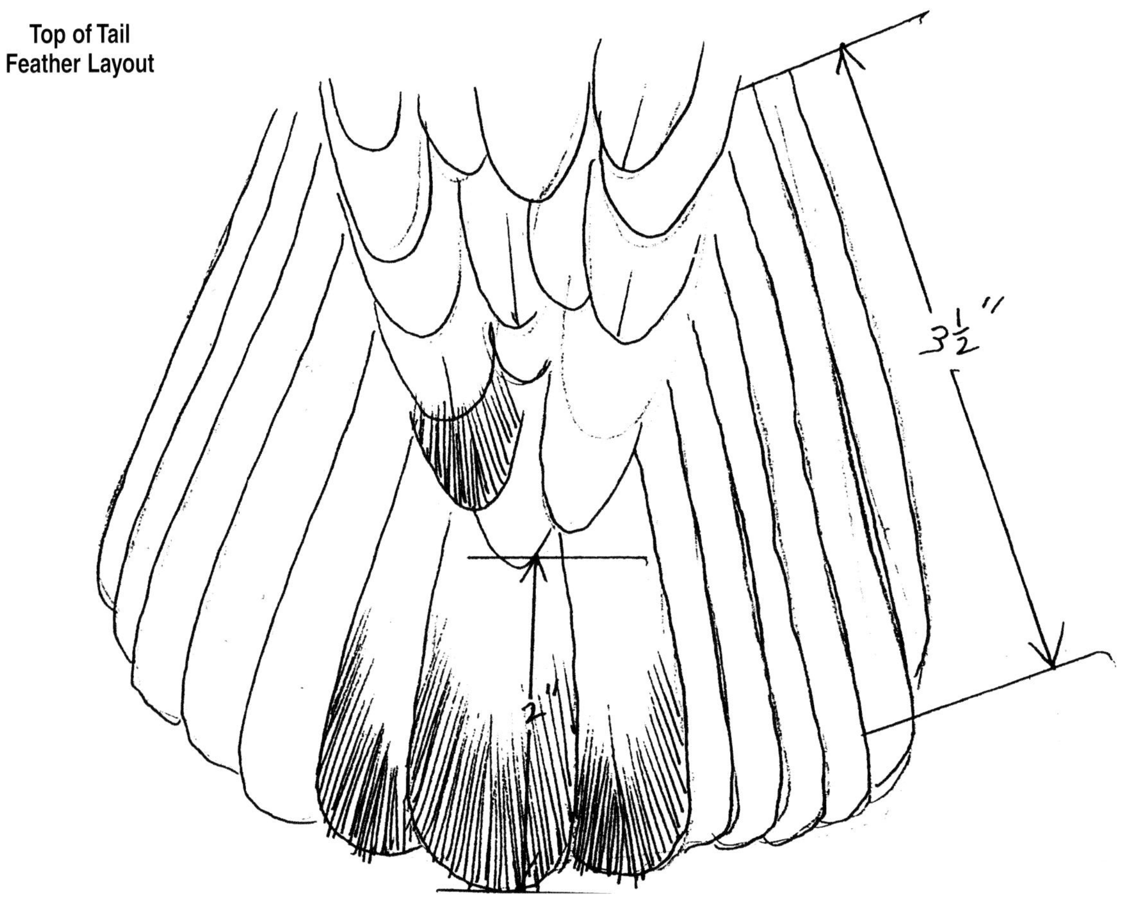

Underside of Tail

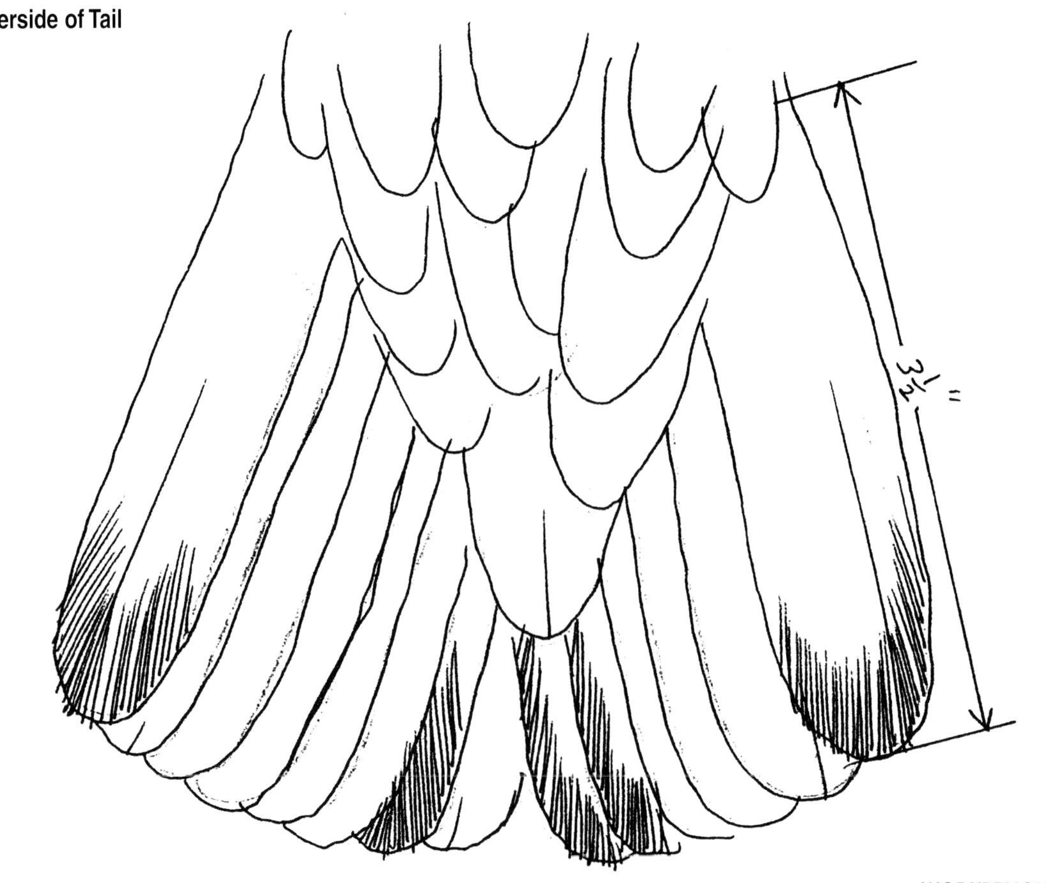

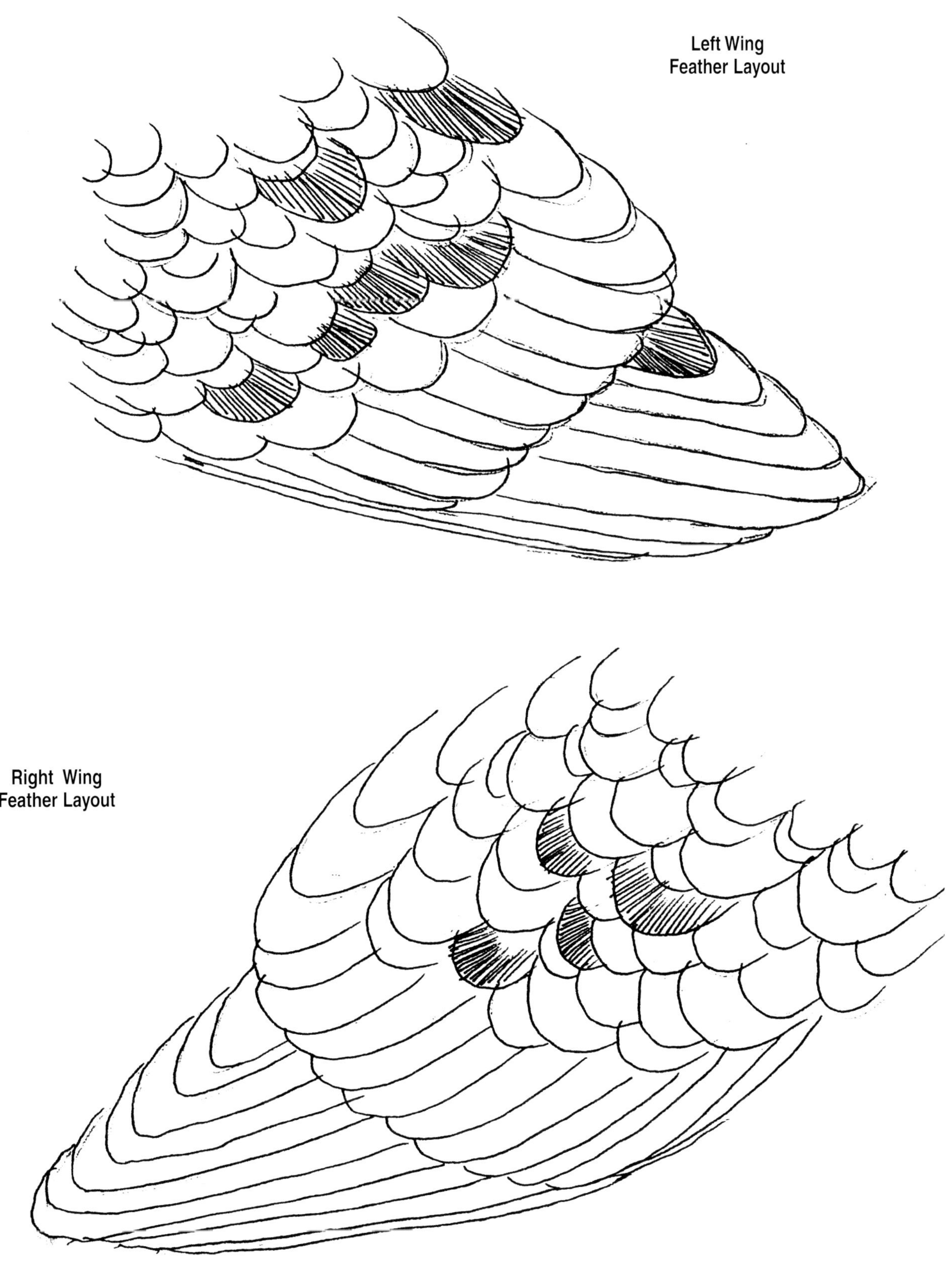
Left Wing
Feather Layout
Right Wing
Feather Layout

CARVING THE EASTERN RUFFED GROUSE

1 If you can get your hands on a study skin of your subject you will be ahead of the game in terms of both feather identification and color, and the anatomy of such tricky areas as the feet. Study skins can be obtained from museums and taxidermists, or found for sale at large wildfowl events such as the Ward World Championship.

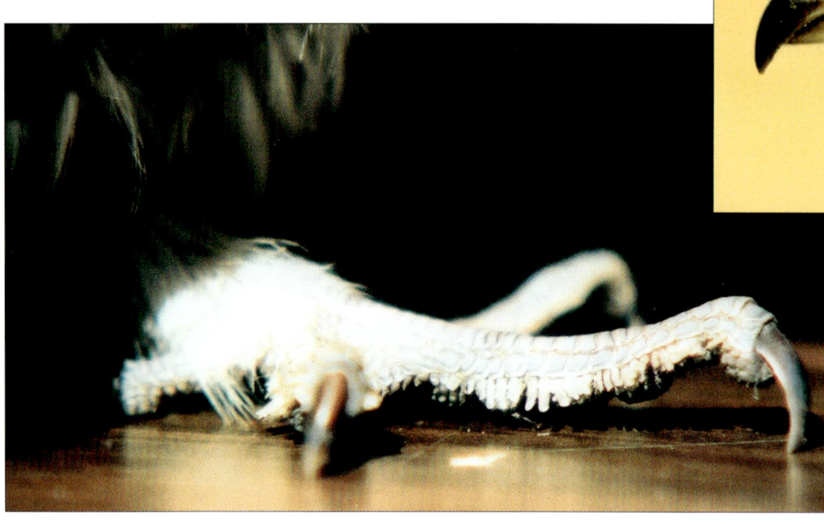

2 Bandsaw the initial grouse cutout from a piece of tupelo or other carving wood using the side and top view patterns on pages 57 and 58.

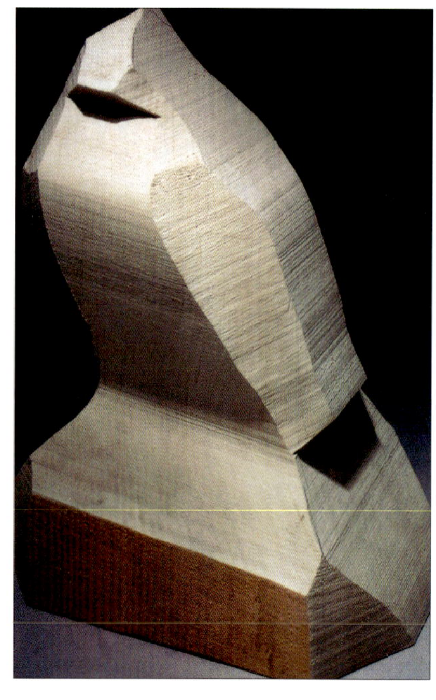

3 Draw a centerline from the tip of the bill to the top of the head, and sketch in the bill in pencil as seen here.

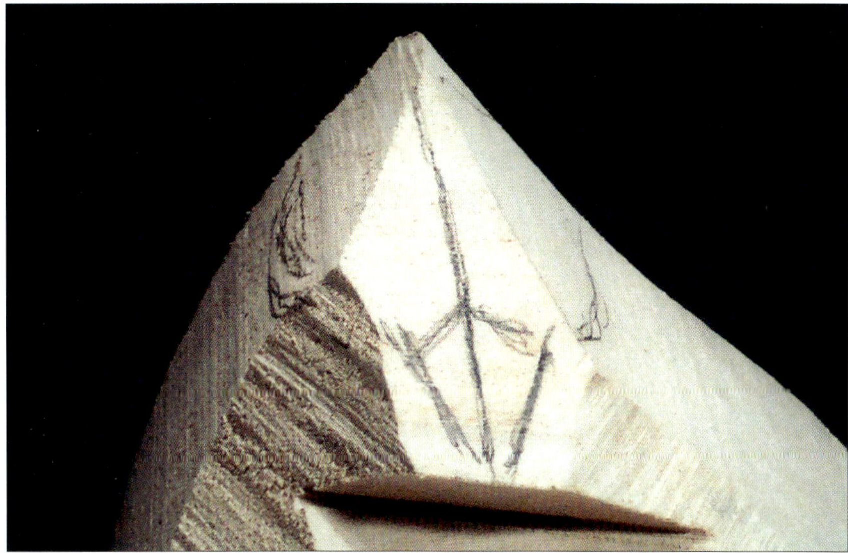

4 Begin to shape the bill and the head with a stump-cutter in your micromotor grinder.

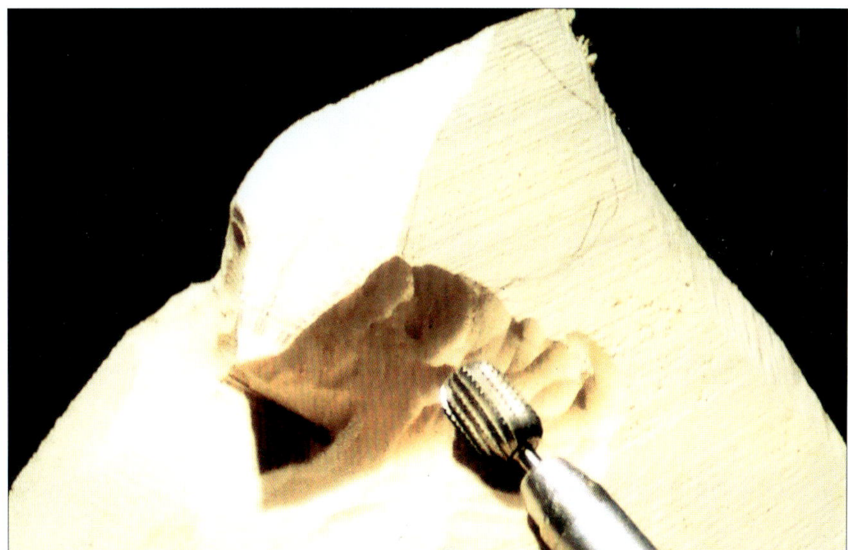

5 Pencil in and carve the grouse's eye channel with the same tool, removing wood slowly and carefully and paying close attention to your reference.

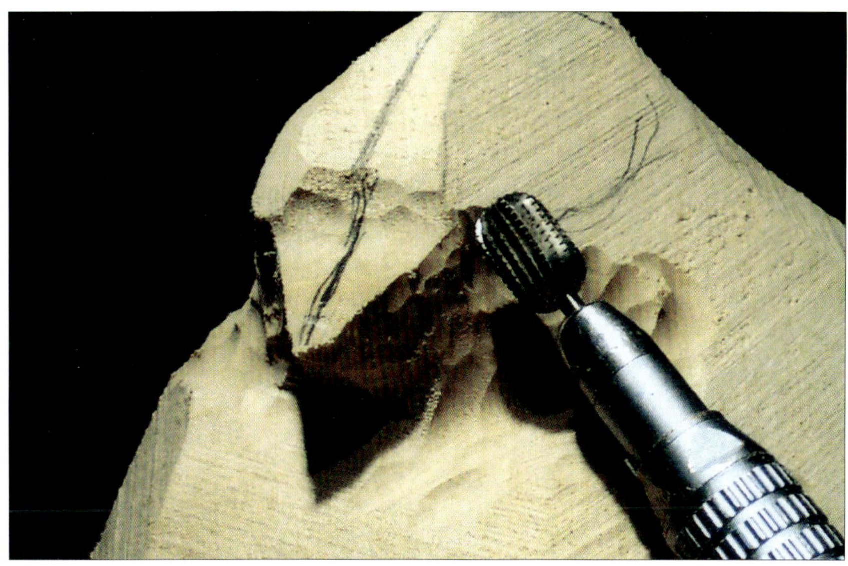

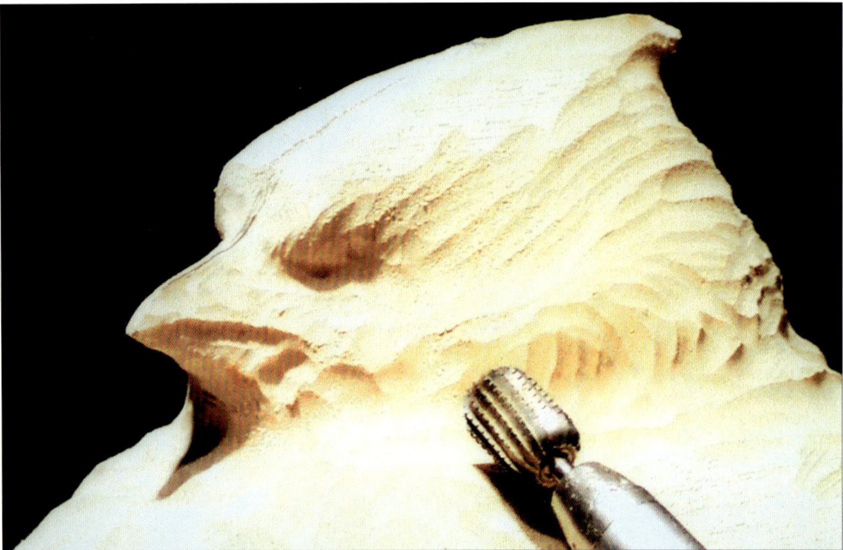

6 Continue to shape the head with the stump-cutter. In addition to making sure that you are anatomically accurate in this area, you can really project the attitude of the bird by tilting or turning the head or carving an open or closed eye. Pay attention especially to the muscle groups and bulges around the eyes on the ruffed grouse.

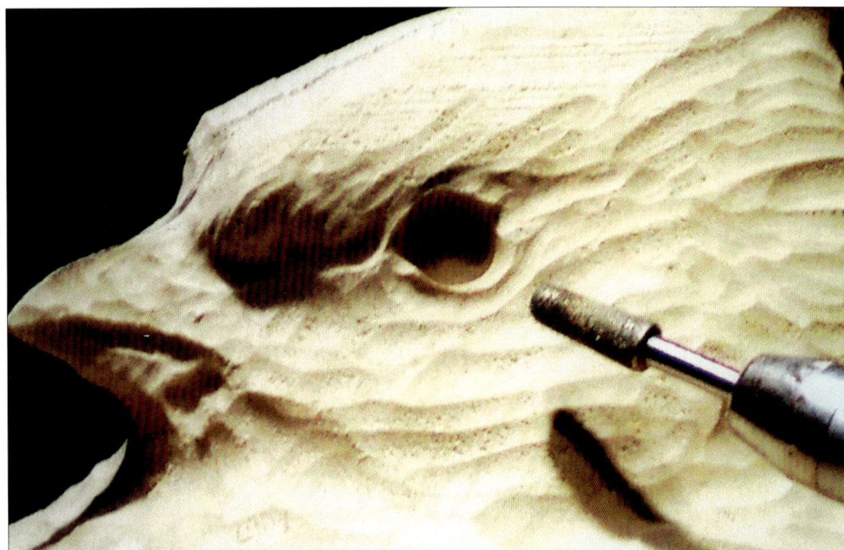

7 Carve out the grouse's eye sockets with a diamond bullet cutter. The eye sockets should be deep enough so that the eye is visible from a direct-line, front view.

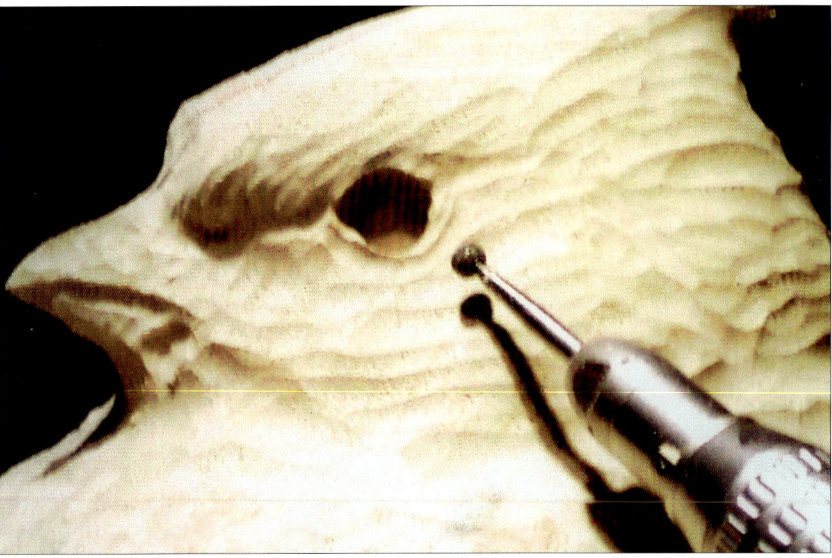

8 Use a diamond ball cutter to carve the inner eyelid.

9 Insert the glass eyes as you did on the previous two birds.

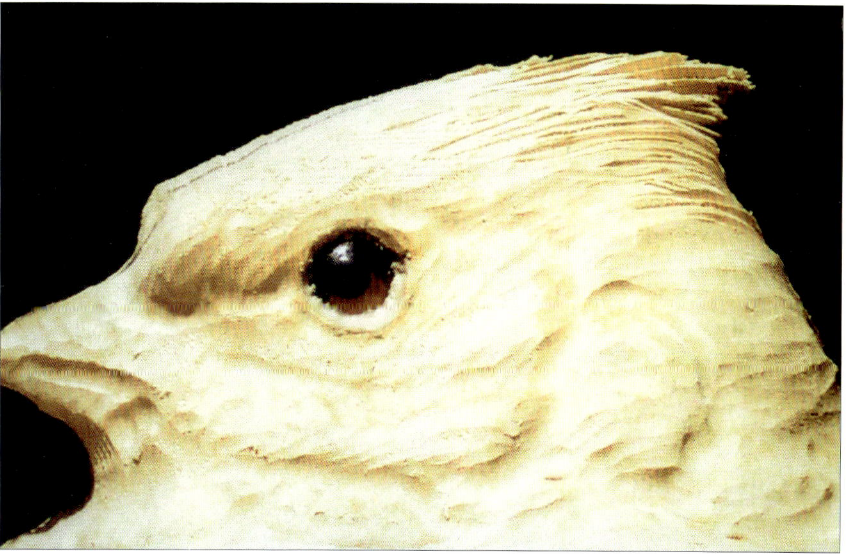

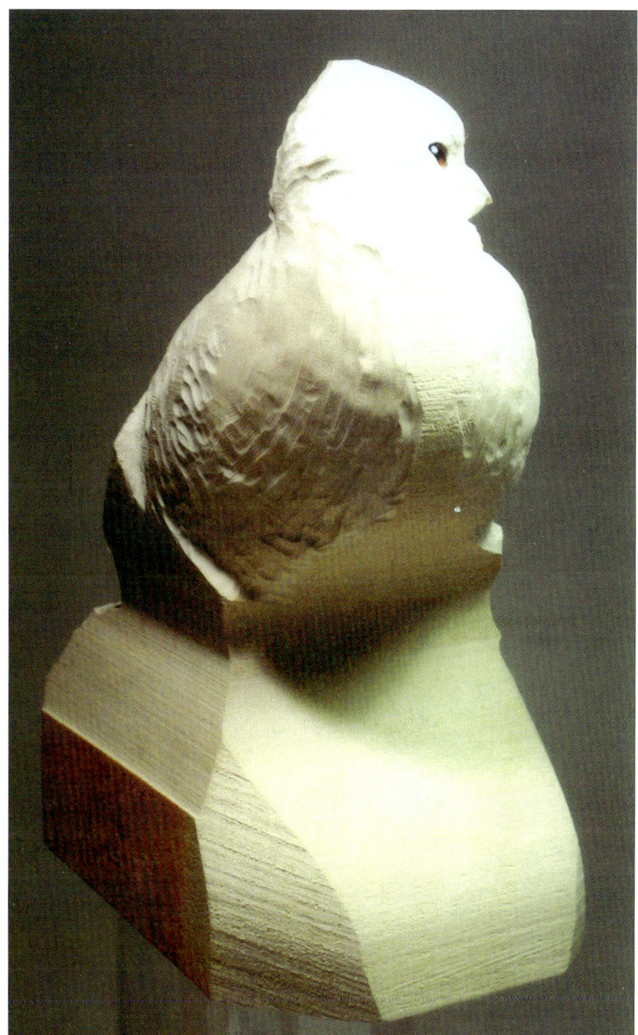

10 Rough-shape the body of the grouse with a stump-cutter according to your reference material.

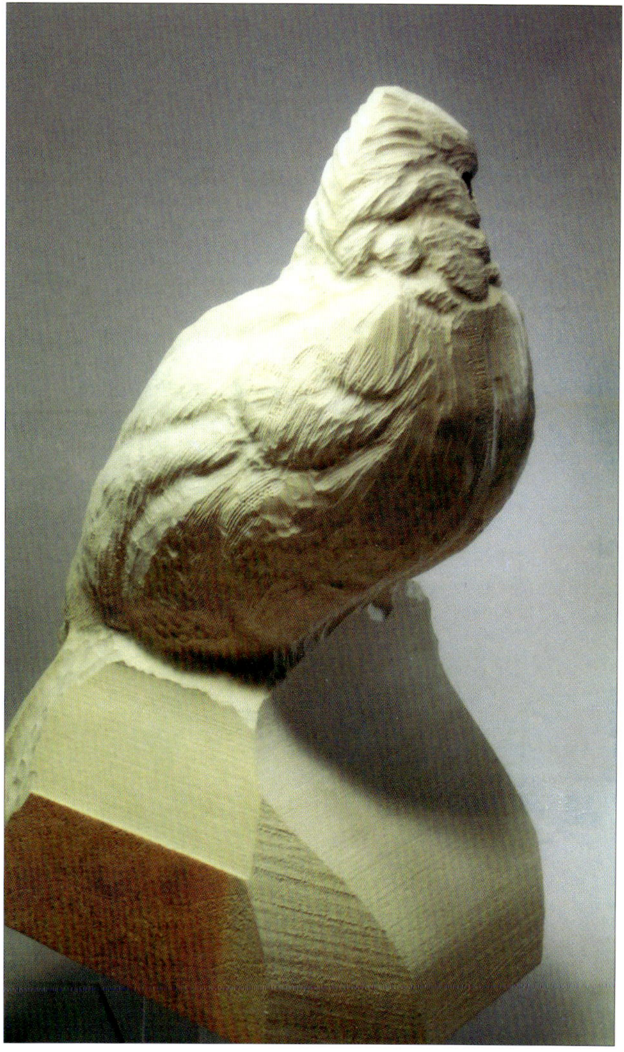

11 Bring the head and wing-feather groups down to size with the stump-cutter.

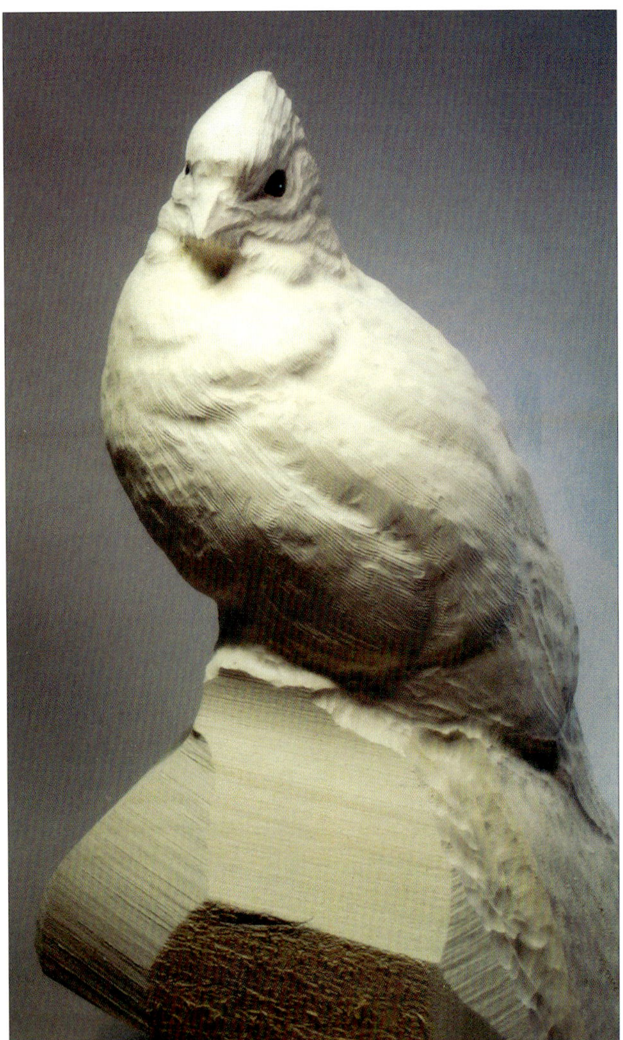

12 Here is a front view of the contoured ruffed grouse. The decision of which muscle groups to accentuate is completely at the discretion of the carver, who must decide what attitude he or she wants to portray. The study of reference photos can help greatly in this area by illuminating the common stances and tendencies of the subject species.

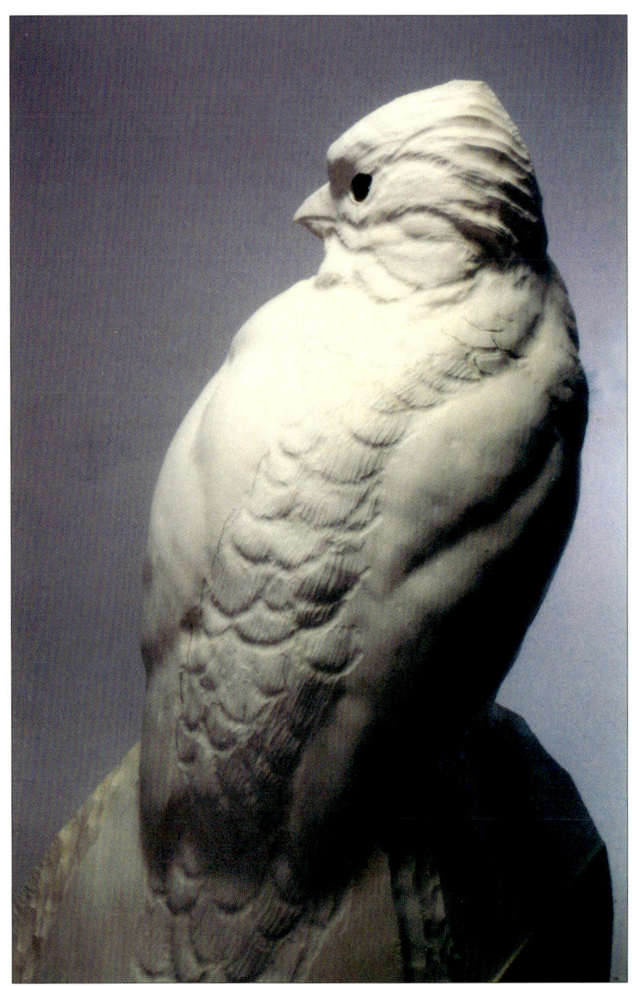

13 Carve the feathers of the cape, scapulars, and coverts. These feathers can be carved in several different ways. One method is to use a bent, blunt burning tip to shape their outlines. Another approach is to carve the outline of the feathers with a tapered white stone and then sand the ridges smooth.

BURNING AND PAINTING THE EASTERN RUFFED GROUSE

1 Here is the sequence of steps for burning and painting a ruffed grouse feather.
a. First, pencil in the feather outline.
b. Burn the feather according to your sketch.
c. Paint gesso in-between the burn lines.
d. Paint the center of the feather (using Burnt Umber in this case).
e. Here is a real quail feather, the appearance you are striving for.

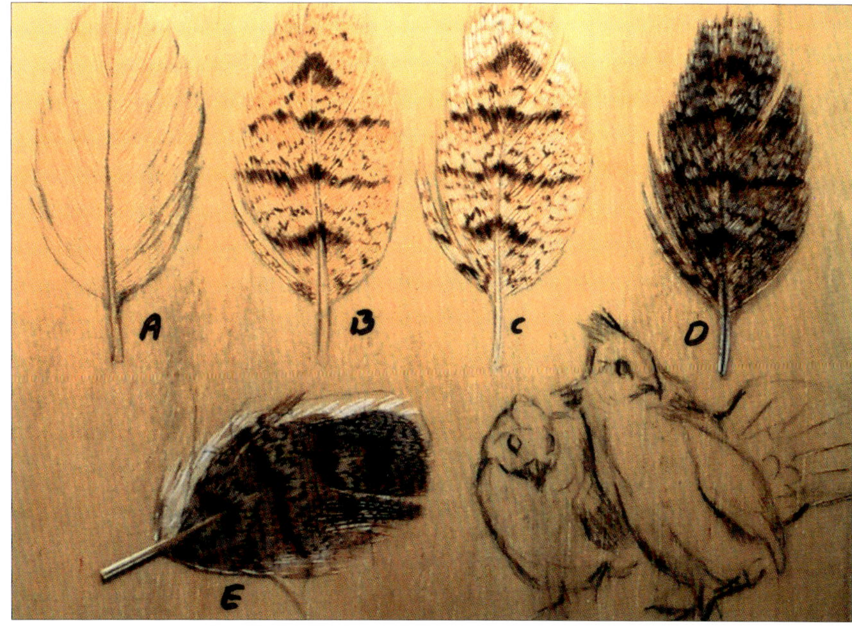

2 This flat carving illustrates the types of individual feathers needed to create a ruffed grouse, and their locations within the feather groups. Burn the feathers on your bird as you see them here, after practicing the individual feathers on some scrap wood.

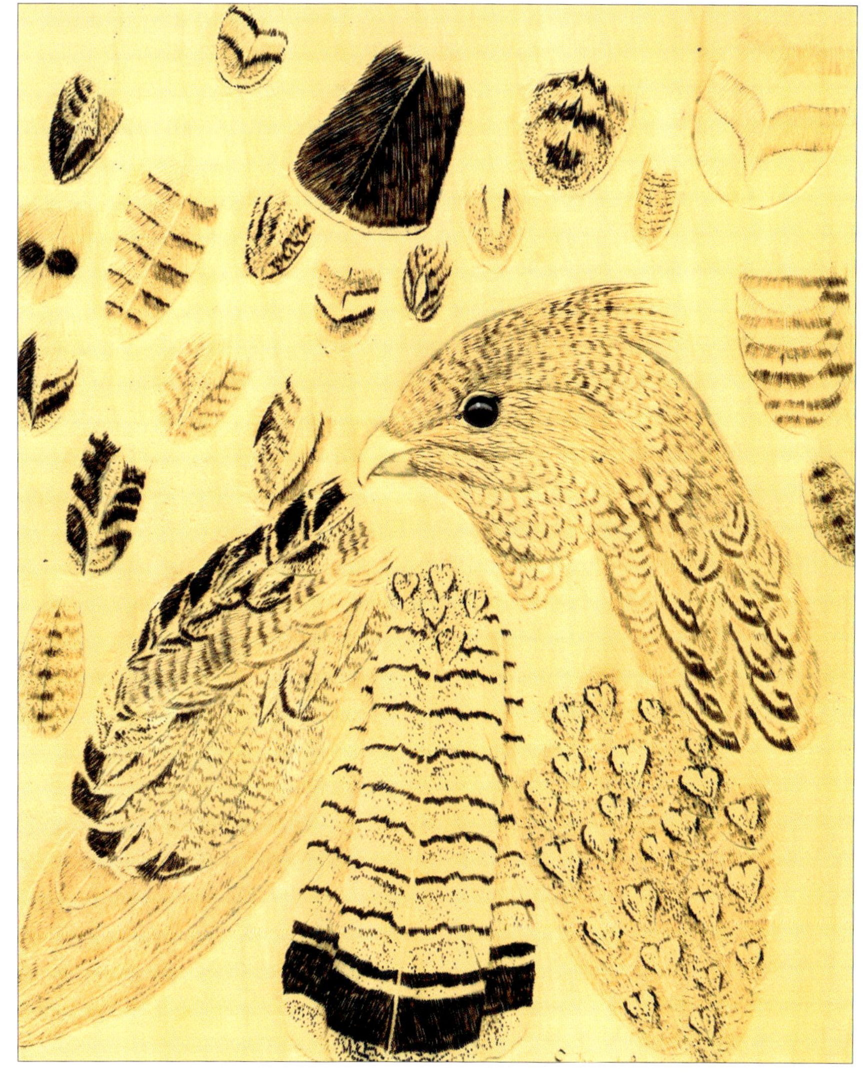

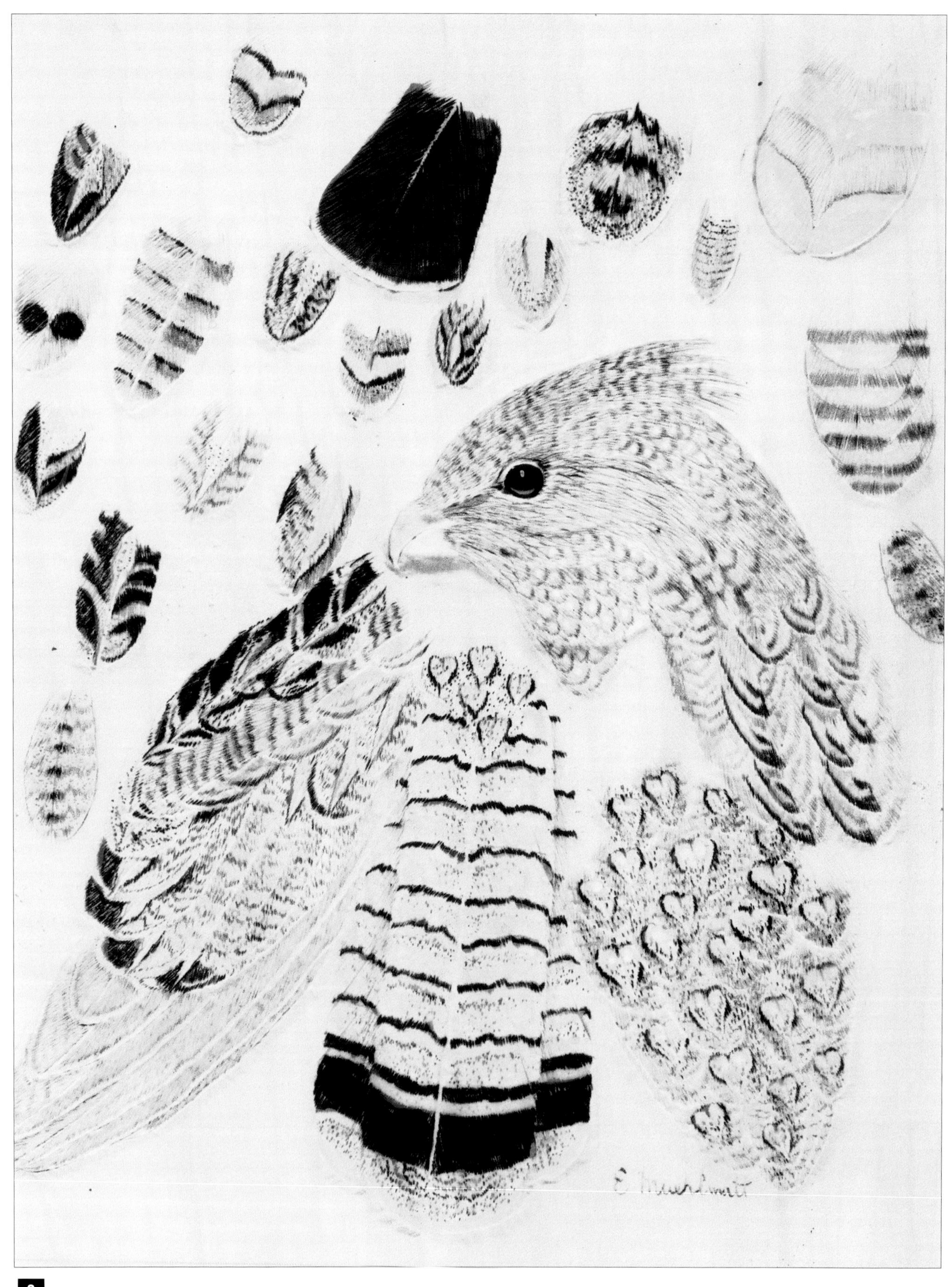

3 After you have burned all of your feather groups, apply gesso to the light areas of the grouse as seen here.

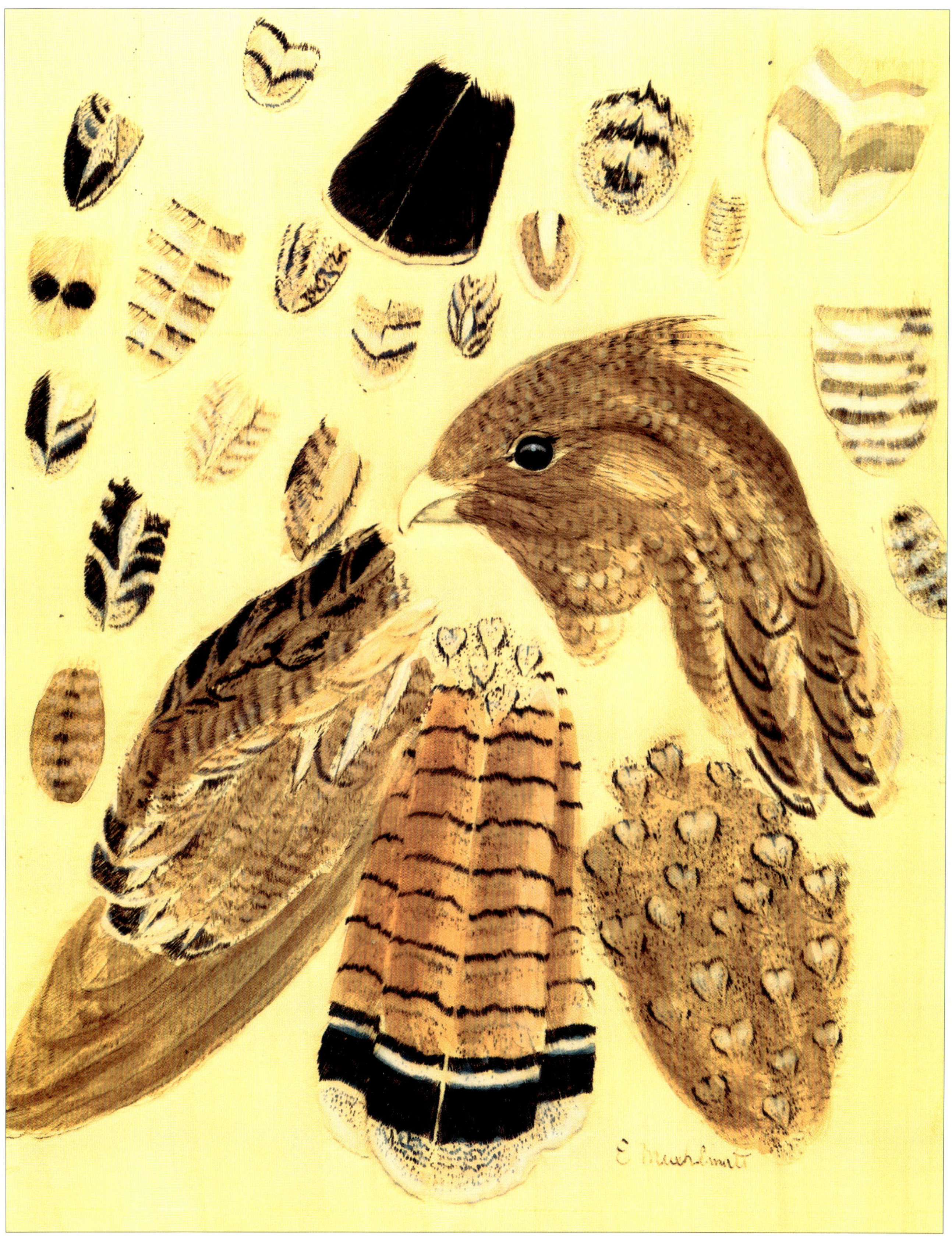

4 Then you can paint the feather groups as shown. Paint the top of the head, cape, wing coverts, and secondaries with a very thin wash of Jo Sonja's Burnt Umber. Then wash the back of the neck, cape, and chest with a thin dilution of Liquitex Bronze Yellow. The tail may be painted with a thin wash of a mixture of Jo Sonja's Raw Sienna and Burnt Sienna. Use Burnt Umber for the primaries, which will require several washes.

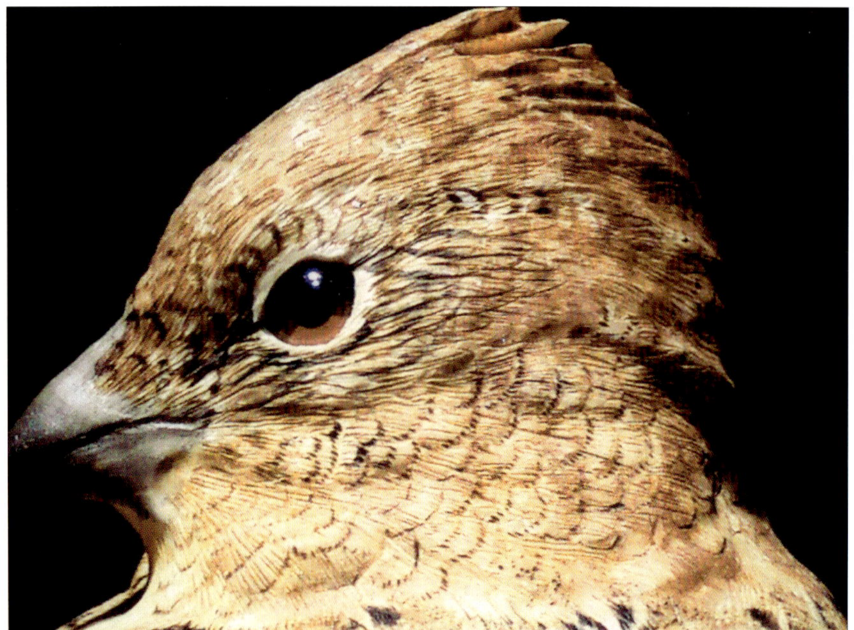

5 Here is a close-up of the completed head of a ruffed grouse. The feather tips were burned and thin washes of Burnt Umber were applied to build up color. I touched-up a few of the feather tips with a 50/50 mixture of gesso and water, and also painted the area under the beak with this color. The heavily burned areas beneath this white area were painted with Warm Black.

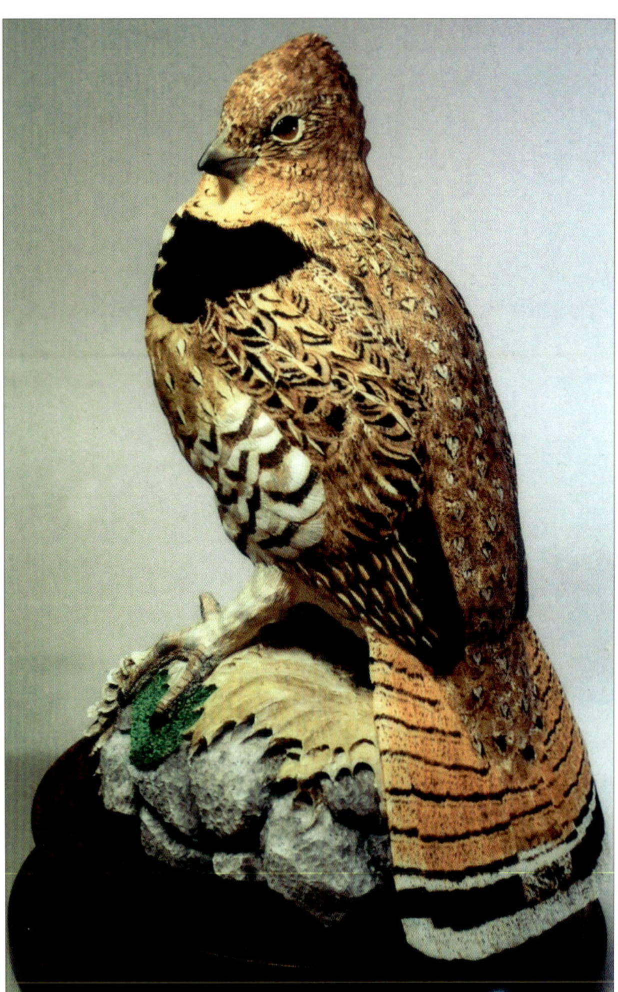

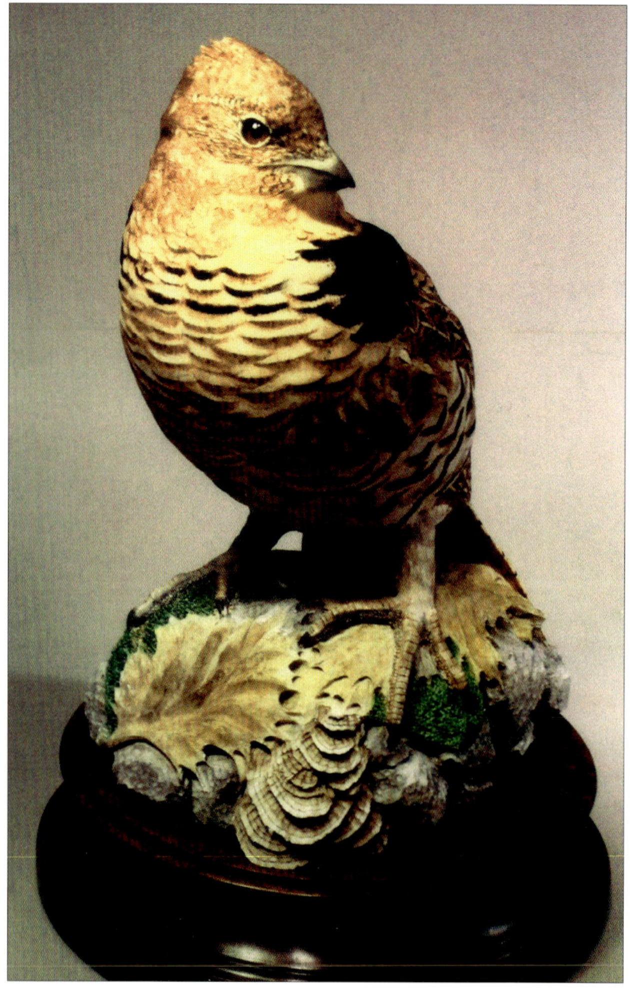

6 Here is the completed ruffed grouse sculpture with all of the feather groups painted.

7 You may alternatively choose to present the grouse in a seated, resting position as seen here.

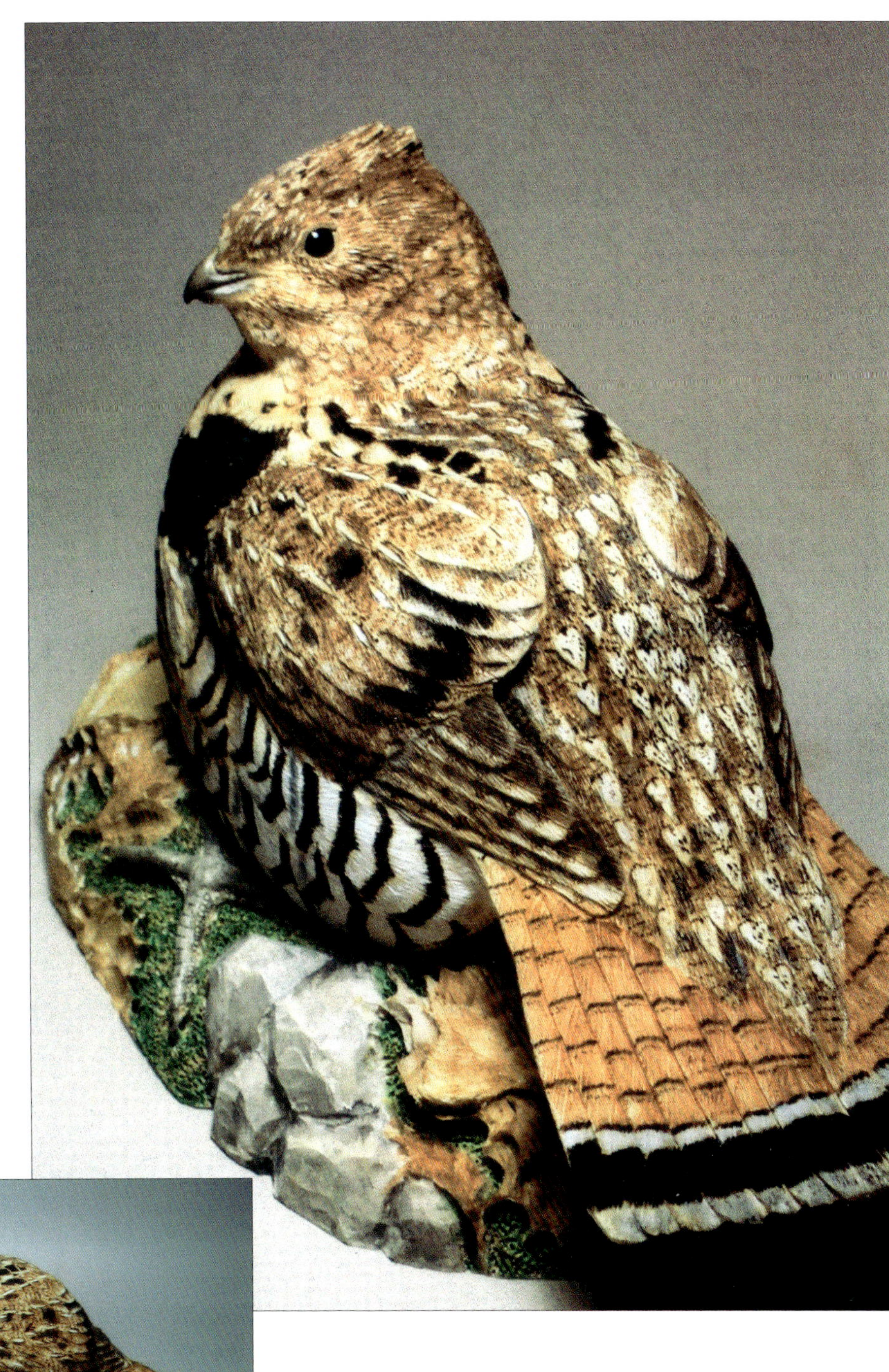

REFERENCE PHOTOS

American Woodcock

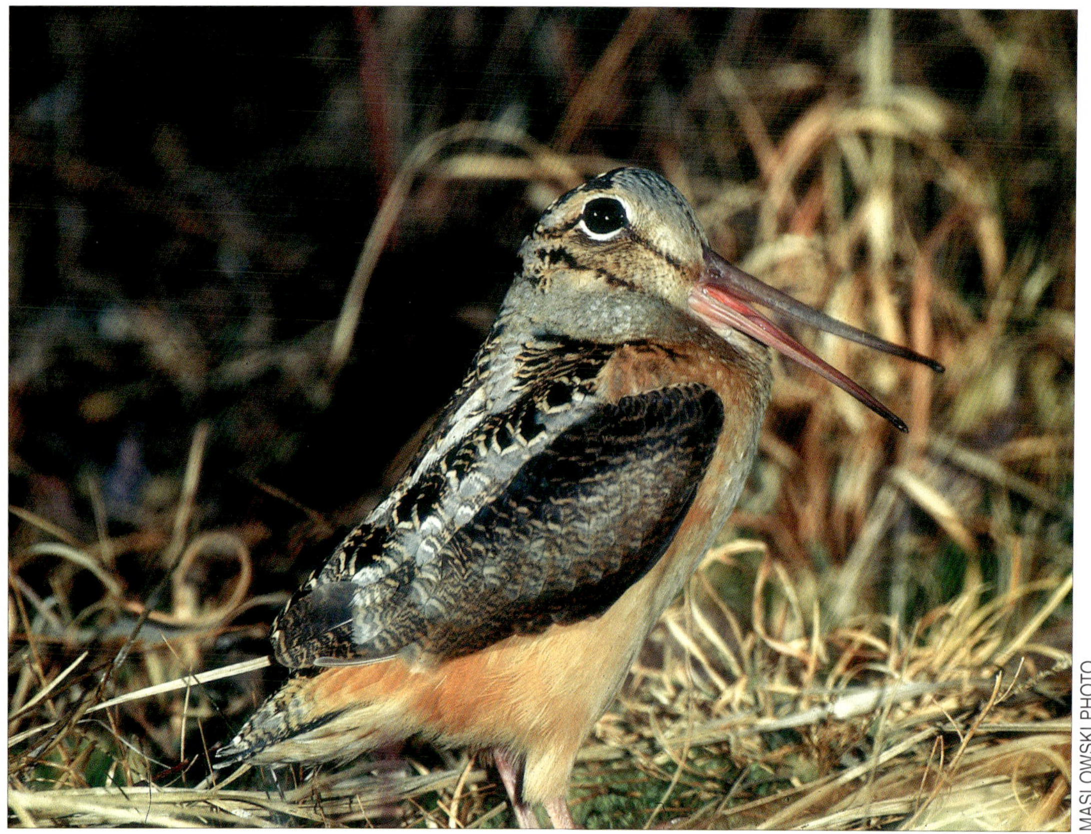

MASLOWSKI PHOTO

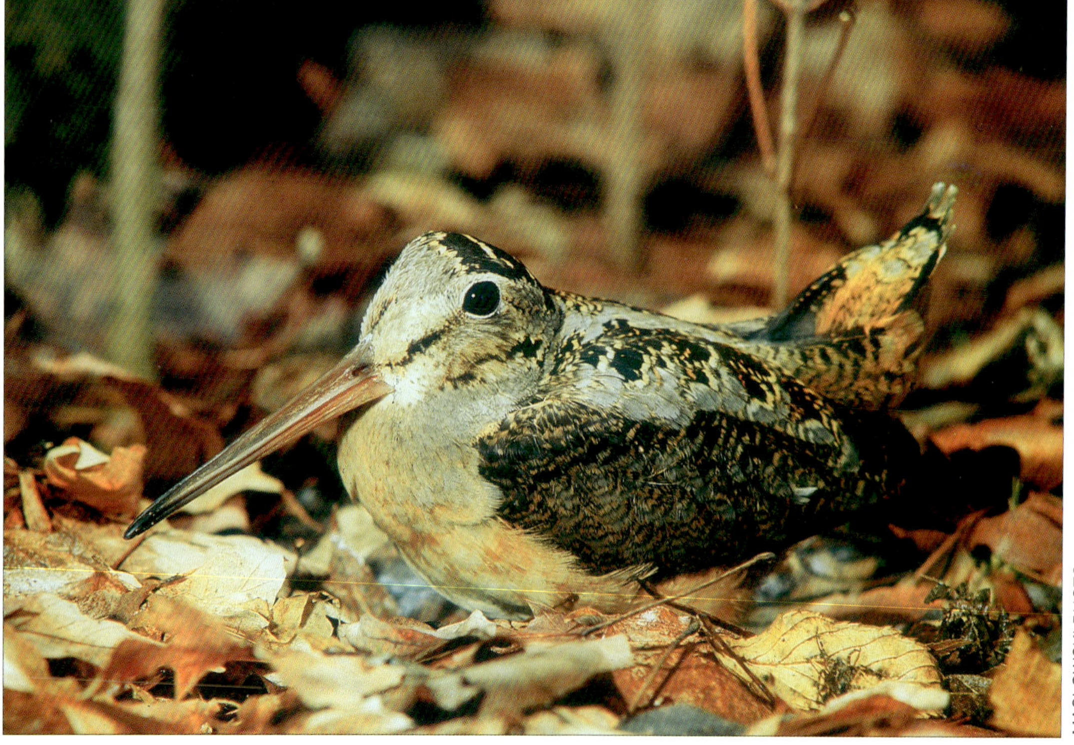

MASLOWSKI PHOTO

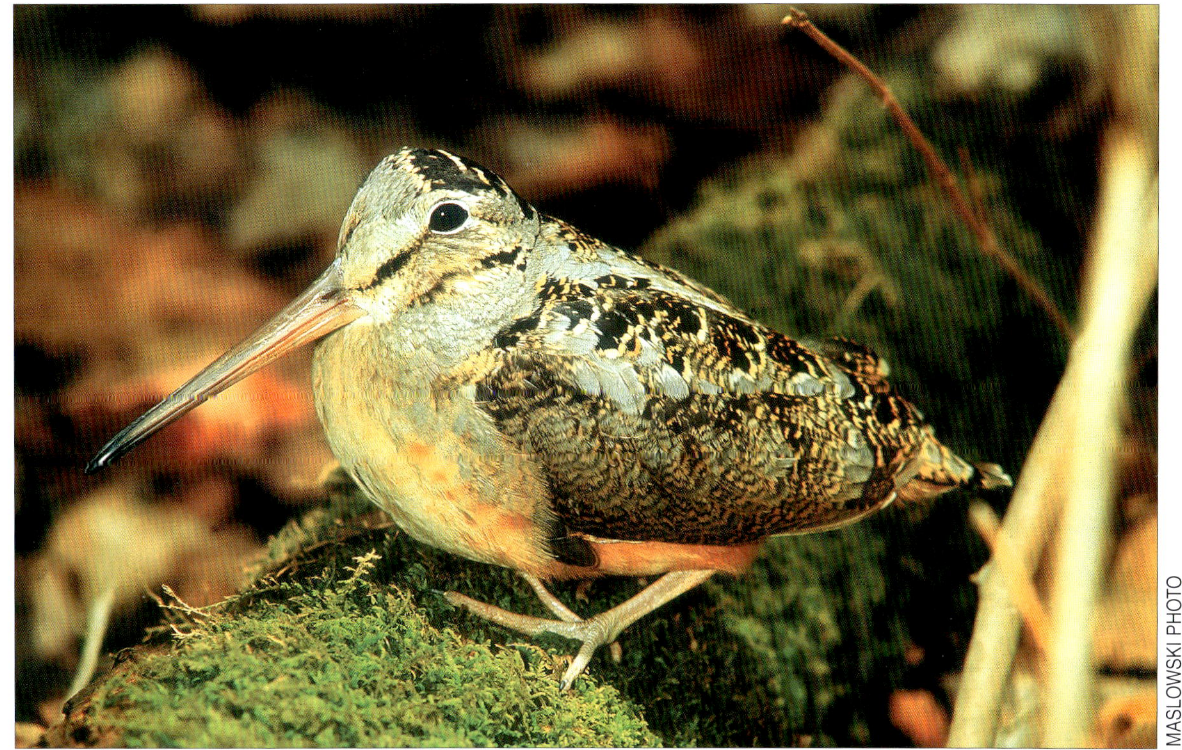

MASLOWSKI PHOTO

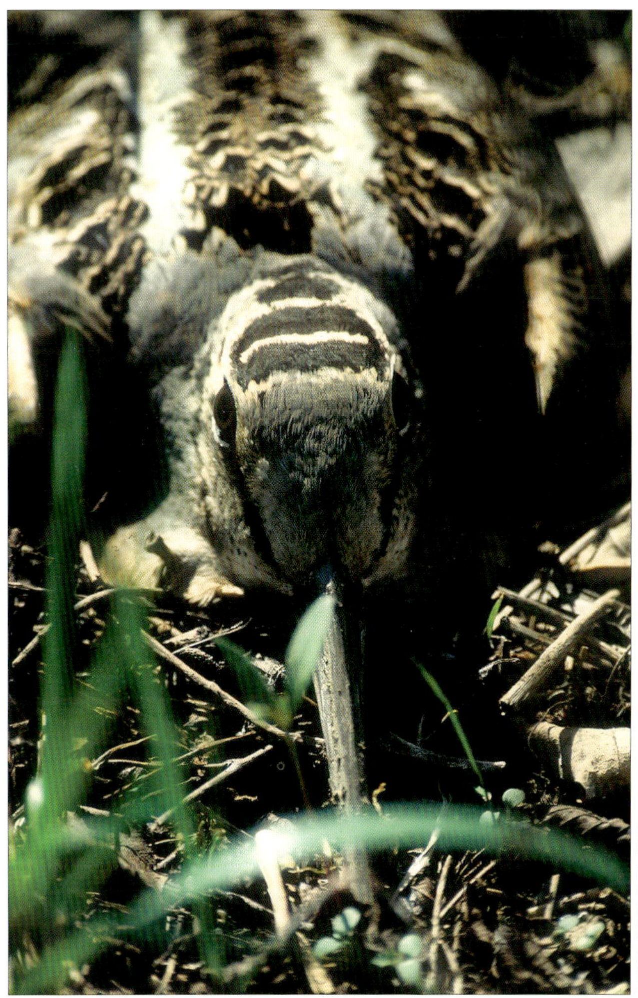

MASLOWSKI PHOTO

Northern Bobwhite

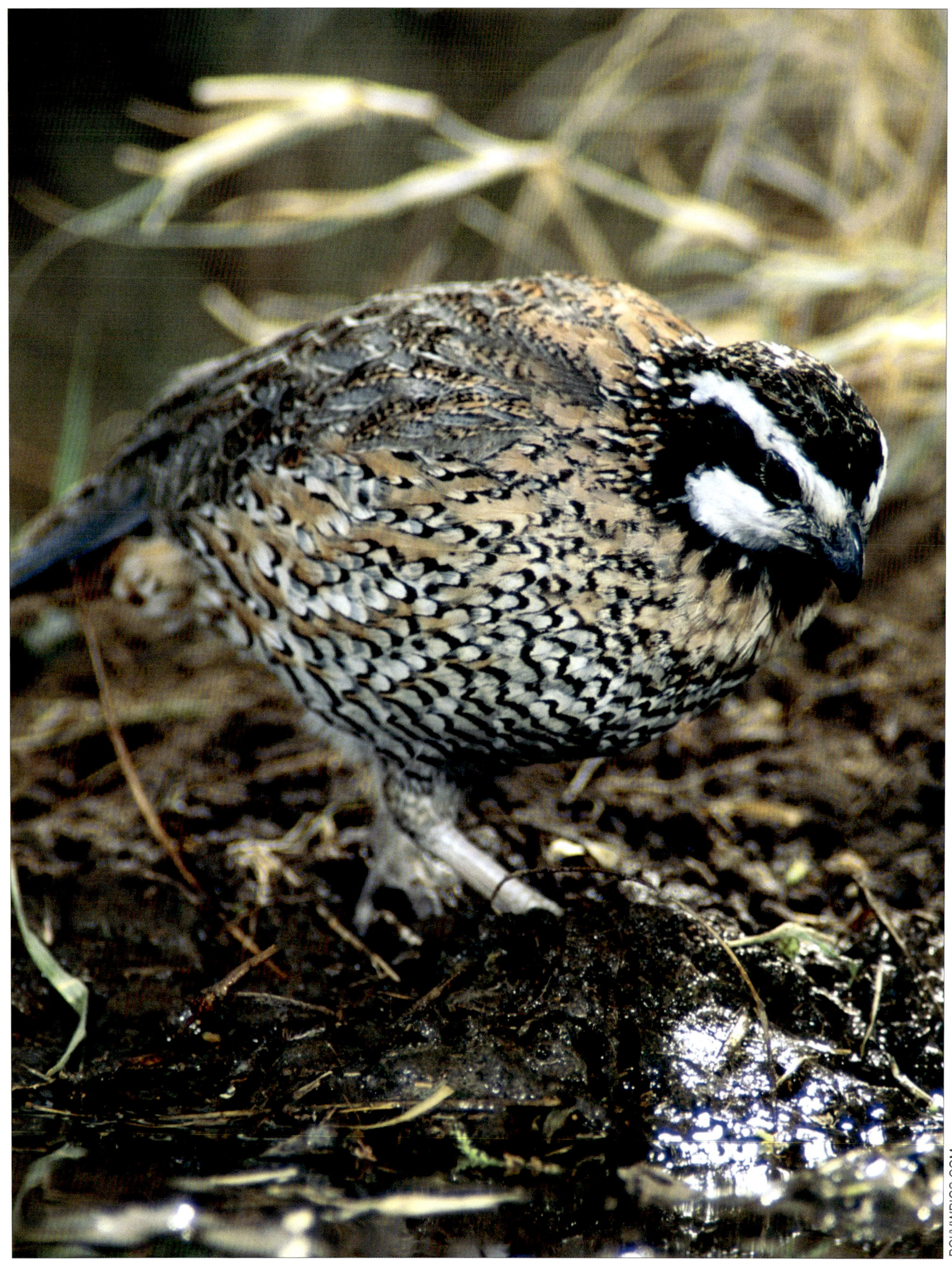

BCI/VWPICS.COM

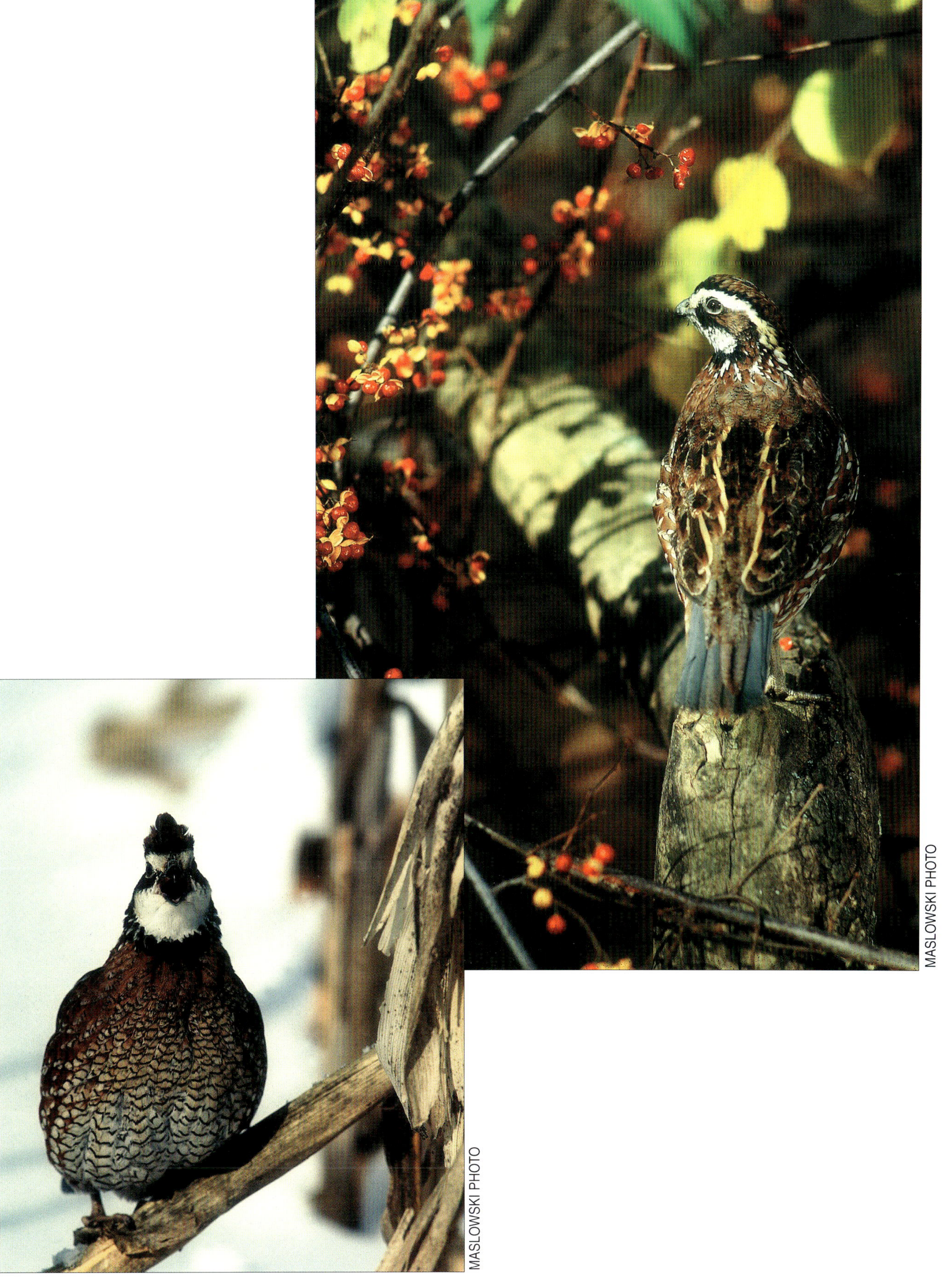
MASLOWSKI PHOTO
MASLOWSKI PHOTO

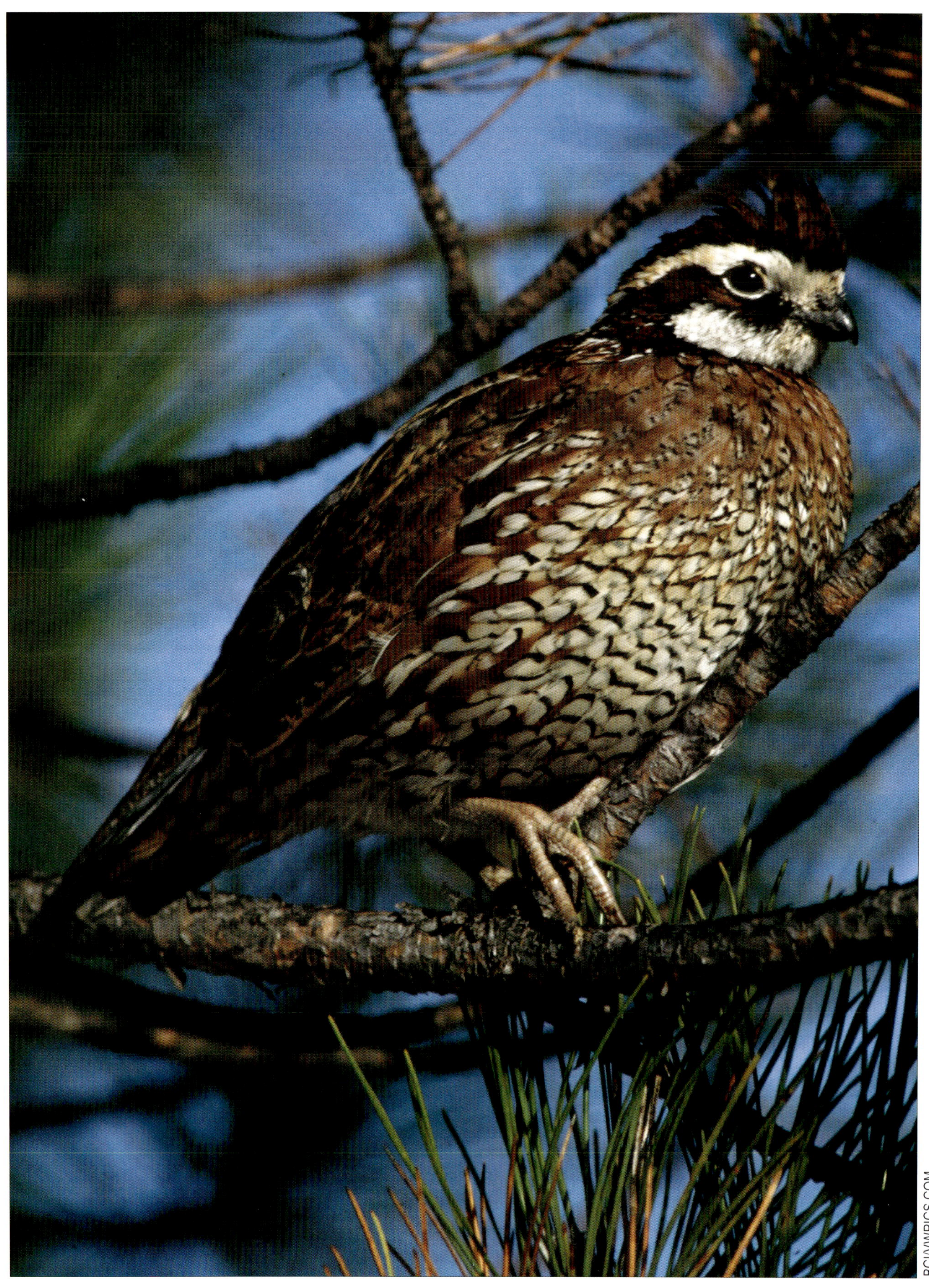

BCI/VWPICS.COM

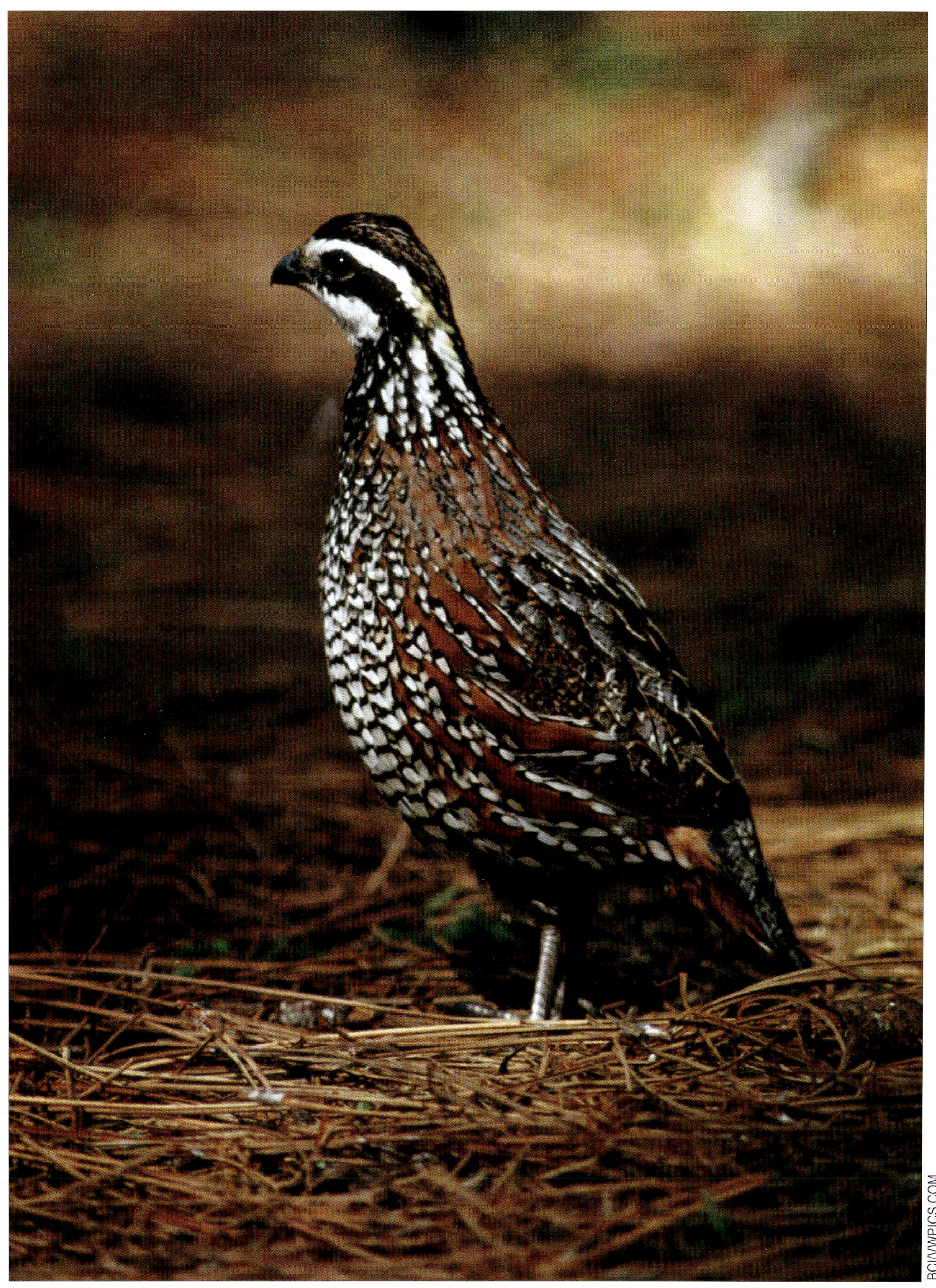

BCI/VWPICS.COM

Eastern Ruffed Grouse

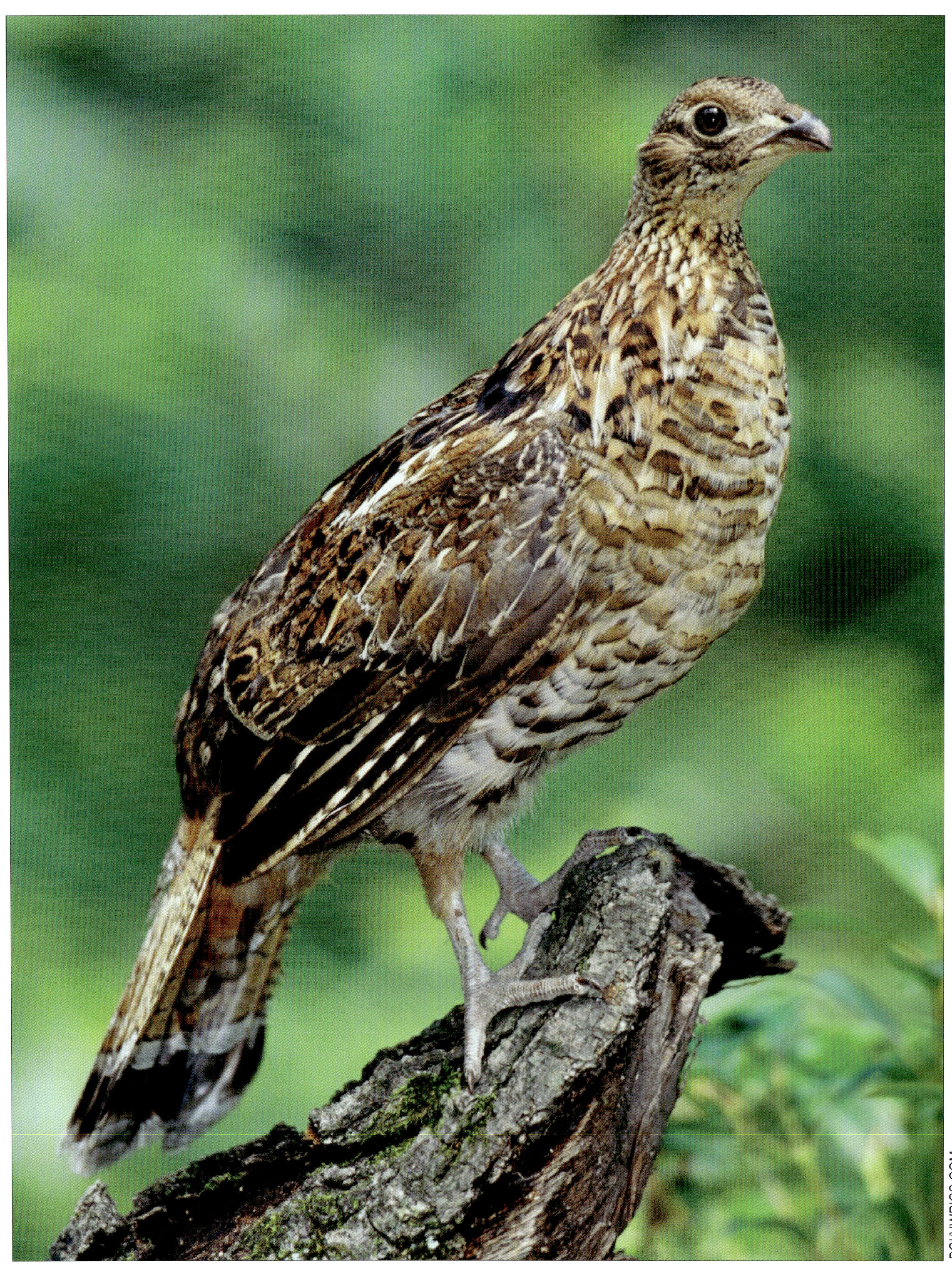

BCI/VWPICS.COM

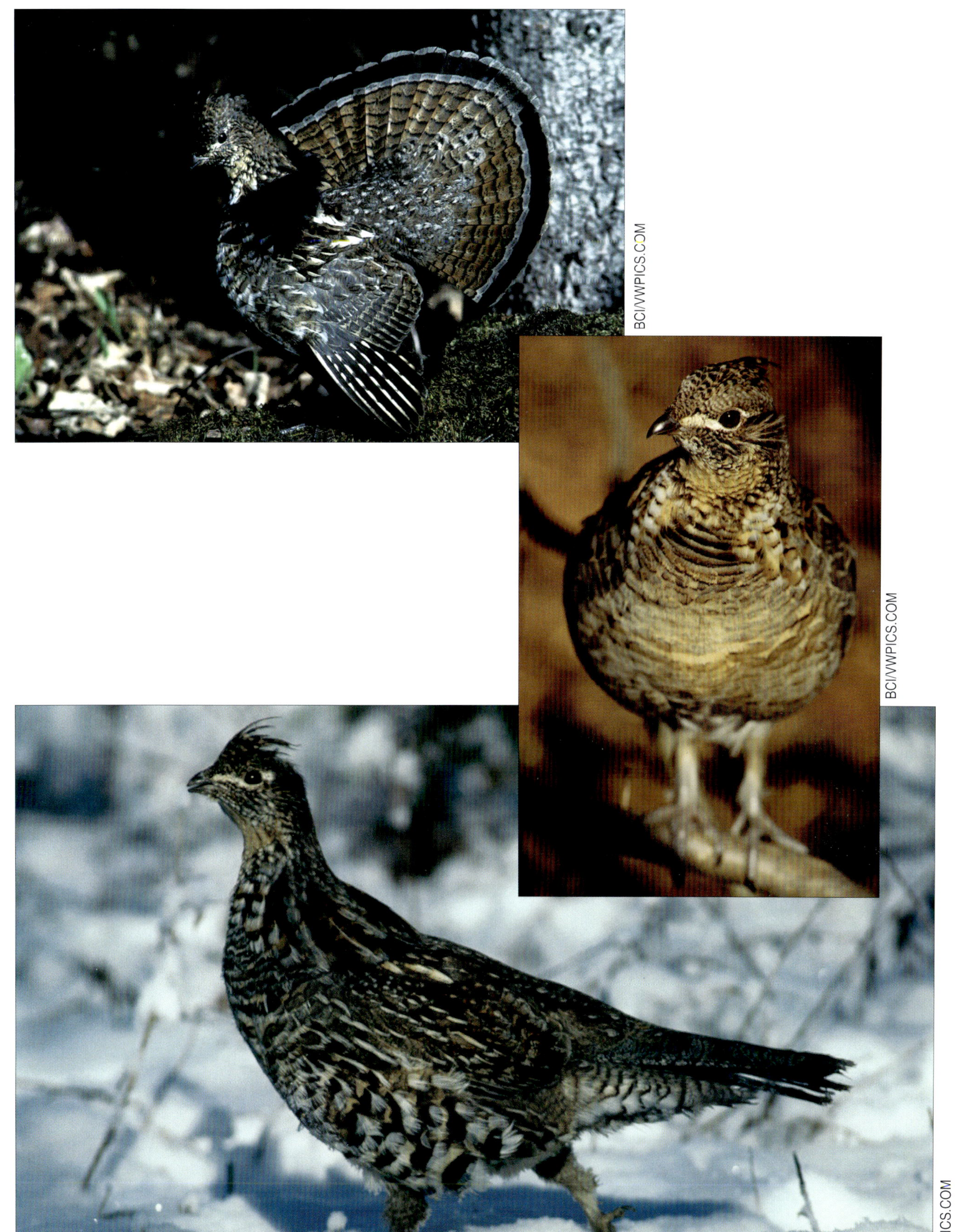
BCI/VWPICS.COM
BCI/VWPICS.COM
BCI/VWPICS.COM

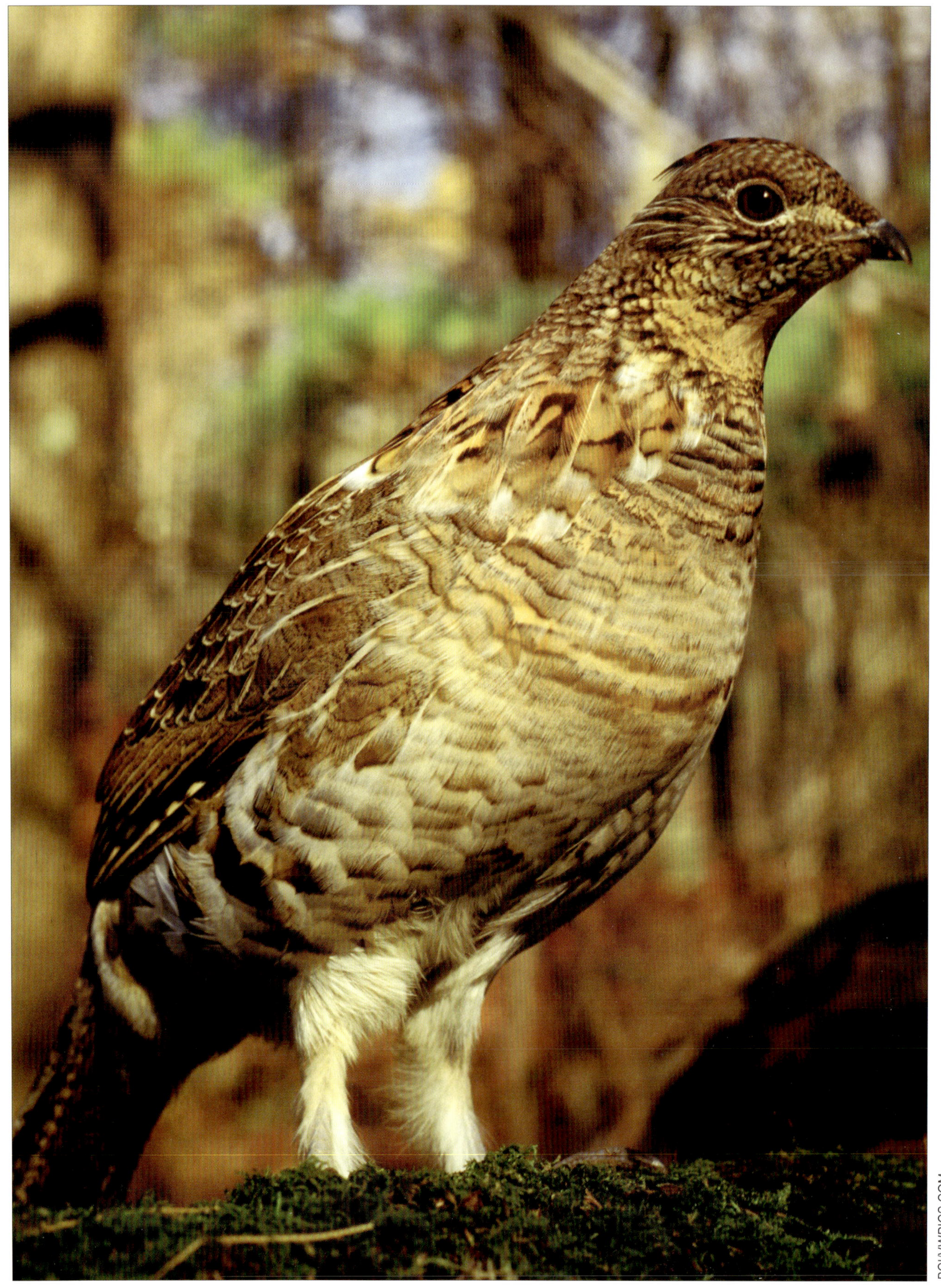

BCI/VWPICS.COM